Army Service Records
of the
First World War

Simon Fowler
William Spencer
Stuart Tamblin

PRO Publications

10th East Yorkshire Regiment marching to the trenches, near Doullens, 28th June 1916. (Imperial War Museum Q 743)

Army Service Records
of the
First World War

Simon Fowler
William Spencer
Stuart Tamblin

2nd edition: revised and updated by William Spencer

PRO Publications

PRO Publications
Ruskin Avenue
Kew
Richmond
Surrey
TW9 4DU

Contents

Illustrations

Front cover: Lieutenant Alfred Bland, formerly of the Public Record Office, killed in action 1 July 1916. (PRO 8/55)

10th East Yorkshire Regiment near Doullens, 28th June 1928. (Imperial War Museum Q 743)

Back cover: A Corporal of the 10th Battalion, Gordon Highlanders, Western Front, 1917 (Imperial War Museum Q 6102)

Using the PRO

Most of the records described in this guide can be consulted at the Public Record Office, Ruskin Avenue, Kew, Richmond, Surrey, TW9 4DU. The Office is open between 9.30am and 5pm Mondays, Wednesdays and Fridays, 10.00am to 7.00pm on Tuesdays, 9.00am to 7.00pm on Thursdays and 9.00am to 5.00pm on Saturdays. The PRO is closed on Sundays, public holidays, and for annual stocktaking. The PRO's website address is:

http://www.open.gov.uk/pro/

The Office is about ten minutes' walk from Kew Gardens Underground Station, which is on London Transport's District Line, as well as the North London Line. For motorists it is just off the South Circular Road (A205). There is adequate parking.

Getting access to the records is simple. You will need to obtain a reader's ticket, which is free, when you first arrive. Please bring some form of identity, such as a driving licence. If you are not a British citizen you should bring your passport.

It is possible to get photocopies of most documents you find: please ask the staff for details. There is a public restaurant and a well stocked bookshop on site. Self service lockers are available to store your belongings. You will need a £1 coin for the lockers.

In order to protect the documents, each one of which is unique, security in the reading rooms is tight. You are only permitted to take a notebook and any notes into the reading rooms. You must also only use a pencil. Eating, drinking and of course smoking are not allowed in the reading rooms.

The PRO can be a confusing place to use. If you are new to the Office it is a good idea to allow plenty of time to find your feet. The staff are both knowledgeable and friendly, and are happy to help if you get lost. You might also want to spend a few minutes watching the introductory video which offers simple advice on how to find the records you want.

Records are normally kept together according to the department which created them. The vast majority of records which relate to the British Army are in the War Office or WO lettercode. Within the lettercode each collection, or class, of records is assigned a separate class number. Thus most War Diaries for the First World War are in class WO 95. It is these class numbers which are referred to throughout this guide.

Brief descriptions of every document (piece is the term used by the PRO) are in the class lists. Several sets of lists are available in the Research Enquiries Room and other locations. The class list gives you the exact reference of the document you want. This is what you order on the computer terminal. Occasionally in this Guide we use the full reference, which is written thus: WO 95/5467.

An increasing number of documents are available on microfilm or microfiche. Where this is the case the fact is noted in the text. You do not need to order microfilms on the computer as you can help yourself to them in the Microfilm Reading Room.

Preface to the Second Edition

As the records of service for soldiers who saw service in the First World War continue to be released, so the number of records available has increased. New information has been added about the 1998 releases of Officers' service records, together with further advice which to help you identify relevant records more easily.

Preface to the First Edition

November 1996 saw the first public access to some of the surviving service records from the period of the First World War. These remarkable records are the most important sources for the study of this war to be made available for many years.

This short guide offers a preliminary introduction to these records and the other sources held by the Public Record Office (PRO) which may help you trace your ancestor's service in the British Army between 1914 and 1920. It also briefly covers the chief sources which are to be found elsewhere. It is intended to produce similar guides to service records of the other armed services in the First World War.

The book is very much a collaborative effort between the three authors: Simon Fowler, William Spencer, and Stuart Tamblin. Simon Fowler wrote the sections about the First World War service records, other non-medal sources at the PRO and sources outside the PRO. William Spencer was responsible for the section on medals, and Stuart Tamblin produced the worked examples based on researches for material on his great-uncle and wife's great-grandfather, as a genealogist's rather than a military historian's view of the sources.

The authors acknowledge the assistance provided by Lesley Wynne-Davies of the Friends of the PRO, Pam Ray of the Australian War Memorial, Andrea Duncan, Roderick Suddaby and Gwyn Bayliss of the Imperial War Museum, Professor Ian Beckett of Luton University, Joe Kelly of the Ministry of Defence, Christopher Staerck, Aidan Lawes who commissioned the book, and Melvyn Stainton, Millie Skinns and the rest of the publishing team who saw it through the press.

They shall grow not old as we that are left grow old:
Age shall not weary them, nor the years condemn.
At the going down of the sun and in the morning,
We will remember them.

Laurence Binyon, *For the fallen* (September 1915)

Chapter 1: Service Records of Other Ranks

1.1 War Office Series – Other Ranks (WO 363) – the 'Burnt Documents'

Service records for other ranks whose Army service ended between 1914 and 1920, that is for men who were either non-commissioned officers or ordinary soldiers, are being gradually transferred from Hayes, where they have been in the custody of the Ministry of Defence, to the Public Record Office at Kew. Before their transfer to the Office they had a chequered history.

The records were originally kept so that the authorities could answer questions about pensions, claims for disability allowances, and queries about entitlements for medals. During 1940 they were badly damaged in a bombing raid and about 60% of the records were totally destroyed.

The vast majority of the surviving records suffered badly from both fire and water damage. Known, naturally enough, as the Burnt Documents, they contain records for about 25-30% of the men who served in the British Army during the First World War. There is thus a one in three or one in four chance of finding a soldier's record. They are at present stored in 33,000 boxes on 3.2km of shelving, each box containing between 840 and 1200 items, at the Ministry of Defence site at Hayes, Middlesex.

The Public Record Office has received a grant from the National Heritage Lottery Fund for a pilot project to see whether it is possible to microfilm these documents and how long it might take. If this is successful, and further funds are forthcoming, it is hoped that the microfilming project should be complete by the end of 2001.

It is a huge project to undertake, which is made even more difficult by the poor state of the documents. **Because of the fragility of the original documents it will never be possible to allow public access to the originals.** A sample page, showing evidence of burning, is reproduced as fig 19.

The Office will make the burnt records available on microfilm as they are filmed - the whole collection will not be available for at least five years. As the records are filmed they will be put into the record class WO 363.

At the time of writing (December 1997) only surnames beginning with the letter Q, U, V or Z have been released. Letters O and N should be released before June 1998. Unlike WO 364 which is arranged in one numerical sequence (WO 364/1 beginning with surnames starting with A and WO 364/4912 beginning with surnames starting with Z), WO 363 is arranged by individual letter, with each letter of the alphabet having its own numerical sequence starting at 1. The records in WO 363 are not in absolutely strict alphabetical order and it is therefore necessary to consult the class list to identify which piece ought to contain the surname you seek. The four letters available at the time of writing are numbered WO 363 Q/1-36, WO 363/U1-45, WO 363 V/1-122 and WO 363 Z/1-5.

Unlike WO 364 which only contains records for those individuals who survived their service, the records in WO 363 contain files of those individuals who were killed in action, died of wounds or executed, as well as those who survived their service.

WO 363 Z	Names from	Names to
1	Zabiela Alfred	Zander Arthur C
2	Zander Ernest A	Zeff Louis
3	Zehnder Alfred B	Zimmerman Bernhardt
4	Zimmerman Charles	Zurhorst Frederick G
5	Zusman E M	Zyczynski W

For a fee of £20, the Ministry of Defence will search the records still remaining at Hayes. This service is now available to anybody, not just next of kin which used to be the case. They normally provide a typed summary of the record sheet, but will provide photocopies if asked to. **Until further notice, all initial enquiries about these records should be directed to the Ministry of Defence, CS(RM)2, Bourne Avenue, Hayes, Middlesex, UB3 1RF.**

Once a letter of the alphabet from both collections (WO 363 and WO 364) is available at the PRO, the MOD will cease carrying out a paid search service on that letter.

1.2 War Office Series – Other Ranks (WO 364) – the 'Unburnt Documents'

To try to remedy the worst effects of the damage, and because the records continued in administrative use, an attempt was made to put together a second collection from duplicates held by the Ministry of Pensions. These were known as the Unburnt Documents, or the "14-20 Collation". This new material added between 8 and 10% to the surviving records, although there is some overlap between the two series, i.e. sometimes a file will be found on the same man in each series. **This series is unlikely to hold any papers for men who were killed in action and had no dependents or who were discharged as part of the demobilisation at the end of the war and could not claim a pension.** It is these 'Unburnt' documents which have been filmed and are now available in class WO 364. In due course, it is hoped to have sets of these microfilms and the finding aids that go with them available in locations other than the PRO but no such arrangements have yet been made. Please see the genealogical press for developments.

It is not possible to say for certain how likely you are to find your man amongst the Unburnt Documents. There is approximately a one in ten chance of doing so. Also included are a few service records for men who had left the Army long before the First World War, but who were receiving pensions into the 1920s.

Research into the unburnt documents suggests that you *may* be more likely to find them for:

- Soldiers who were serving prior to 1914 and whose service finished between 1914 and 1920;
- Soldiers who were serving prior to 1914 and who were medically discharged without seeing service overseas between 1914 and 1920;
- Soldiers who were serving prior to 1914 and were medically discharged having seen service overseas between 1914 and 1920;
- Soldiers who joined between 1914 and 1920 and who were medically discharged without seeing service overseas;
- Soldiers who joined between 1914 and 1920 and who were medically discharged having seen service overseas.

Both the Burnt and Unburnt Documents contain papers for regular soldiers and part-time members of the Special Reserve or Territorial Force who had enlisted before the War. In some cases these papers go back to the 1880s. Both series also contain records for other ranks who served in the Royal Flying Corps, but left before it became part of the Royal Air Force on 1 April 1918.

1.3 Using the 'Unburnt Documents' – how to find your film and obtain a copy

These documents are available on some 4000 microfilm reels in the Microfilm Reading Room. You will have to find the film you want by referring to the class list for WO 364 (the class containing the unburnt documents) which will give you a piece or box number. Copies of the list are available in both the Research Enquiries Room and the Microfilm Reading Room. If you can't find a copy please ask any member of staff. Part of a typical page is reproduced below - in this example, one would expect to find the file on Ronald Colman, if it exists, under the reference WO 364/757, but in fact it is held under the entries for Coleman, in WO 364/742, a useful warning of the danger of accepting names at face value. The microfilm reel reference appears on the left hand side.

WO 364	name	WO 364 GS no
738	Cole, George - Cole, Owen	1735730
739	Cole, Patrick - Cole, William	1735731
740	Cole, William - Coleman, Frederick	1735732
741	Coleman, Frederick - Coleman, Robert	1735733
742	Coleman, Robert - Coles, Frederick	1735734
743	Coles, Frederick - Coley, Daniel	1735735
744	Coley, Edward - Coller, Frederick	1735736
745	Coller, George - Collie, Andrew	1735737
746	Collie, David - Collier, Reginald	1735738

You do not need to order these documents by computer. They are to be found in clearly labelled cabinets in the Microfilm Reading Room. It is a self-service system, so you can help yourself to the film you require, the same system as the one you may be familiar with in the former Census Rooms.

First find a spare microfilm reader. There is a numbered black box to the right of the machine. Put the box in place when you take a film from one of the cabinets. When you have finished with the film put it back in the correct place in the cabinet and return the black box to the microfilm reader. The same system applies if you want to look at any other microfilm or microfiche in the Microfilm Reading Room.

The films are arranged alphabetically in surname order. Within surnames the documents are normally arranged alphabetically in first name order but on occasion records may be slightly out of order. They are not arranged by regiment or regimental number order. Thus the surname Fowler comes after Fowle and before Fowles. Within the Fowlers, John Fowler will appear after James, followed by John A., John A.A., John Aaron, John Alan, John Andrew and so forth.

There are simple to operate microfilm printers in the Microfilm Reading Room. Just follow the instructions. The machines use tokens which can be bought either from machines in the Microfilm Reading Room or from the counter in the Reprographic Orders Service. It is also possible to have pages copied for you. Naturally enough this service is more expensive.

It will help enormously to find the place on the film if you note down the frame numbers on each frame (that is page of document). On some films unfortunately the frame number is too faint to see. You will then need to note down the names on the documents appearing either side of yours so that you can more easily find your place on the film.

The number of microfilm reader-printers is limited. As a courtesy towards other readers please do not hog these machines!

1.4 Standard forms commonly found in the 'Unburnt Documents' series

Each page of the service record has been filmed as it was to be found in the original service record. Nothing has been omitted. Some examples of sample pages are illustrated in figs 1-6, mainly from the file on Ronald Colman, the Hollywood film star. In 1914, he was a shipping clerk who joined up the day after war was declared.

These service records are in effect a collection of forms which were completed for a variety of reasons by Army clerks. The survival rate of these forms is very patchy, and therefore different combinations appear in each record. Much information is repeated, and on occasion, answers to the same question, such as civilian occupation or physical size, may not be consistent within the file.

They are normally arranged with pension records and medical information at the front of each record and miscellaneous correspondence, perhaps about lost records or a mother's plea to let her under-age son be released from the colours, towards the end. There is likely to be very little directly about an individual's war service at the front or anywhere else. You will need to consult the war diaries for the battalion or unit he served with for this information. War diaries are described in more detail in section 2.1 below. A useful list of Discharge documents is reproduced as fig 7.

Some of the more common forms you are likely to come across are:

1.   **Attestation forms** (A.F. B250, B2512, B2056, E501-7) - see fig 1
      This form provides names, regimental number(s), units and ranks, dates and places of attestation, information on age, place of birth and/or address, occupation, physical measurements, and visual description. Also included are details of next of kin, or if the soldier was married, the place and dates of marriage and births of children. The form was regularly updated to provide details of promotions, time served abroad, wounds and decorations awarded. There may be several separate attestation forms if a man served in the Territorial Forces, or even as a regular soldier, before the First World War. The Army form number is given in brackets as an aid to identification.

2.   **Medical history** (A.F. B178, B178a) - see fig 2
      The medical history sheet is divided into four tables. Table I, 'The General Table', was completed at the time of enlistment, and gives an impression of the physical condition of the recruit. Medical grades were included after their introduction in 1916. The table concludes with the dates and reason for the soldier becoming ineffective. Tables II-IV were designed for current use during service. Table II recorded admissions, discharges, and medical treatment in hospitals. Table III gives dates and a brief reference to medical boards, courts of enquiry, recent vaccinations,

and dental treatment. Table IV was rarely used as it was designed to record movements to and from bases.

3. **Casualty Form - Active Service** (A.F. B103, B103-21) - see fig 4
    This form was designed to 'record promotions, reductions, transfers, casualties etc.'. It duplicates to a certain extent Attestation Forms. It is probably the most useful as it gives the most up-to-date information on the next of kin, and a full description of service.

4. **Statement as to Disability** (A.F. Z.22) - see fig 5
    This was completed by all soldiers on demobilization. The first part recorded names, military unit, regimental number, etc. It also included age, date, place of recruitment and medical recruitment when first joined, cause for discharge and prospective address after discharge. When a man was claiming damage to his health due to military service he was asked to provide the following details: Where did he serve? What was his medical complaint and what might have caused it? At which place and date did it originate? The concluding section dealt with his civilian employment with details of his last employer. The information was followed by the opinion of a medical officer who was asked to provide a diagnosis, to state whether any complaint was caused or aggravated by military service, and to assess the degree of disablement.

5. **Medical report on a Soldier Boarded prior to Discharge or Transfer... to the Reserve and Medical Report on an Invalid** (A.F. B179, B179a)
    This form or forms includes judgment of the medical board which re-examined a man prior to his discharge. It includes more about the medical history of the soldier.

6. **Regimental Conduct Sheet**
    This form briefly described those offences which resulted in disciplinary action, stating the nature of the offence, where and when it took place, and the verdict.

7. **Proceedings on Discharge** (B 268, B 268A) - see fig 6
    A form normally at the end of a service record recording the date and place of discharge, the reason why, a physical description, and a brief summary of a man's character.

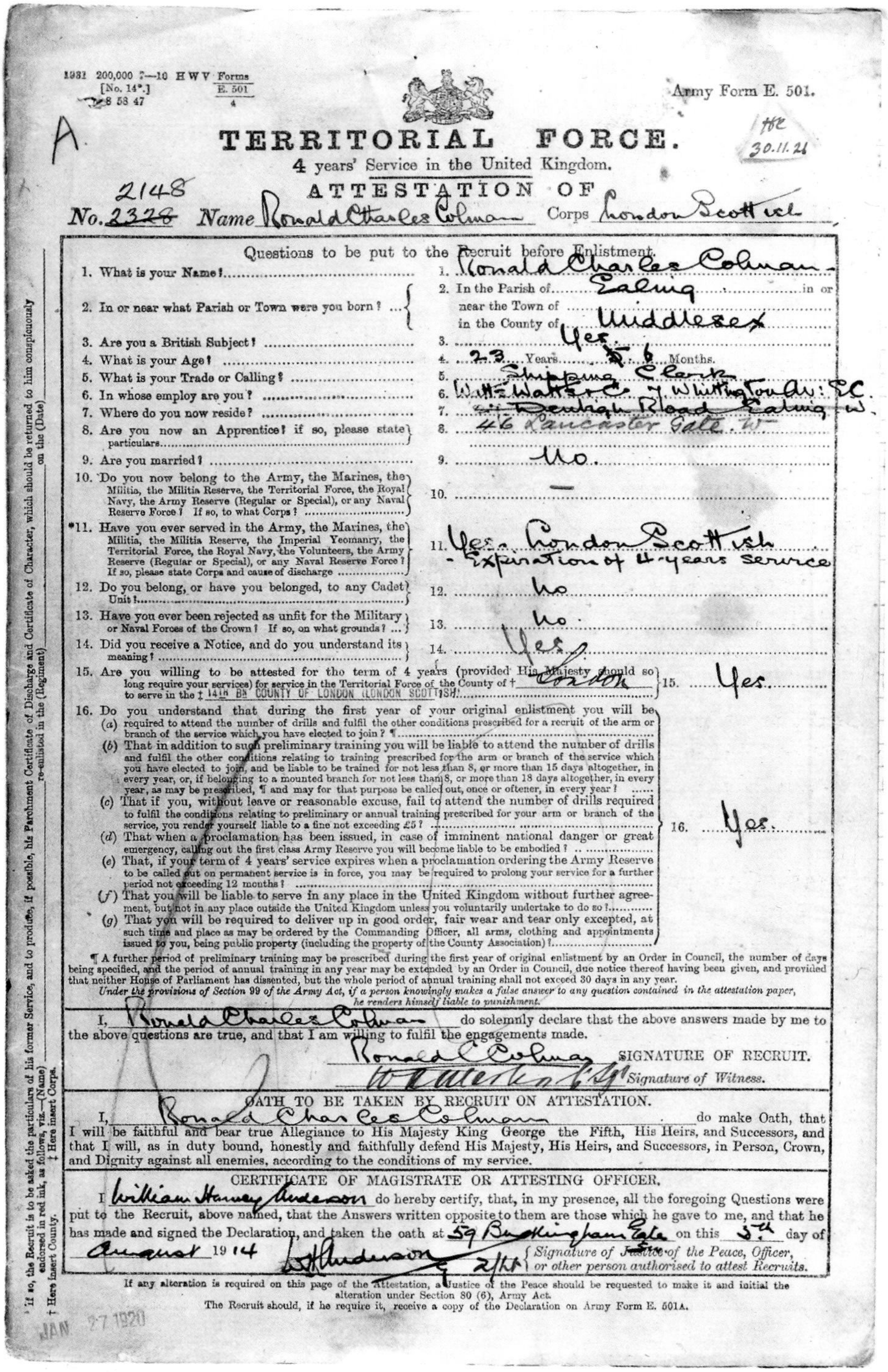

1931 200,000 7—10 H W V Forms
[No. 14*.] E. 501
8 53 47 4

A

Army Form E. 501.

30.11.21

TERRITORIAL FORCE.

4 years' Service in the United Kingdom.

ATTESTATION OF

No. ~~2328~~ 2148 Name Ronald Charles Colman Corps London Scottish

Questions to be put to the Recruit before Enlistment.

1. What is your Name? — 1. Ronald Charles Colman
2. In or near what Parish or Town were you born? — 2. In the Parish of Ealing in or near the Town of ..... in the County of Middlesex
3. Are you a British Subject? — 3. Yes
4. What is your Age? — 4. 23 Years 6 Months.
5. What is your Trade or Calling? — 5. Shipping Clerk
6. In whose employ are you? — 6. Wm Watt & Co 7 Whittington Av: E.C.
7. Where do you now reside? — 7. ~~Denleigh Road Ealing W.~~
8. Are you now an Apprentice? if so, please state particulars — 8. 46 Lancaster Gate W.
9. Are you married? — 9. No.
10. Do you now belong to the Army, the Marines, the Militia, the Militia Reserve, the Territorial Force, the Royal Navy, the Army Reserve (Regular or Special), or any Naval Reserve Force? If so, to what Corps? — 10. —
*11. Have you ever served in the Army, the Marines, the Militia, the Militia Reserve, the Imperial Yeomanry, the Territorial Force, the Royal Navy, the Volunteers, the Army Reserve (Regular or Special), or any Naval Reserve Force? If so, please state Corps and cause of discharge — 11. Yes. London Scottish - Expiration of 4 years service
12. Do you belong, or have you belonged, to any Cadet Unit? — 12. No
13. Have you ever been rejected as unfit for the Military or Naval Forces of the Crown? If so, on what grounds? — 13. No.
14. Did you receive a Notice, and do you understand its meaning? — 14. Yes.
15. Are you willing to be attested for the term of 4 years (provided His Majesty should so long require your services) for service in the Territorial Force of the County of † London to serve in the ‡ 14th Bn County of London (London Scottish) — 15. Yes.
16. Do you understand that during the first year of your original enlistment you will be
(a) required to attend the number of drills and fulfil the other conditions prescribed for a recruit of the arm or branch of the service which you have elected to join? ¶
(b) That in addition to such preliminary training you will be liable to attend the number of drills and fulfil the other conditions relating to training prescribed for the arm or branch of the service which you have elected to join, and be liable to be trained for not less than 8, or more than 15 days altogether, in every year, or, if belonging to a mounted branch for not less than 8, or more than 18 days altogether, in every year, as may be prescribed, ¶ and may for that purpose be called out, once or oftener, in every year?
(c) That if you, without leave or reasonable excuse, fail to attend the number of drills required to fulfil the conditions relating to preliminary or annual training prescribed for your arm or branch of the service, you render yourself liable to a fine not exceeding £5?
(d) That when a proclamation has been issued, in case of imminent national danger or great emergency, calling out the first class Army Reserve you will become liable to be embodied?
(e) That, if your term of 4 years' service expires when a proclamation ordering the Army Reserve to be called out on permanent service is in force, you may be required to prolong your service for a further period not exceeding 12 months?
(f) That you will be liable to serve in any place in the United Kingdom without further agreement, but not in any place outside the United Kingdom unless you voluntarily undertake to do so?
(g) That you will be required to deliver up in good order, fair wear and tear only excepted, at such time and place as may be ordered by the Commanding Officer, all arms, clothing and appointments issued to you, being public property (including the property of the County Association)?
— 16. Yes.

¶ A further period of preliminary training may be prescribed during the first year of original enlistment by an Order in Council, the number of days being specified, and the period of annual training in any year may be extended by an Order in Council, due notice thereof having been given, and provided that neither House of Parliament has dissented, but the whole period of annual training shall not exceed 30 days in any year.

Under the provisions of Section 99 of the Army Act, if a person knowingly makes a false answer to any question contained in the attestation paper, he renders himself liable to punishment.

I, Ronald Charles Colman do solemnly declare that the above answers made by me to the above questions are true, and that I am willing to fulfil the engagements made.

Ronald C Colman SIGNATURE OF RECRUIT.

W Watterton Sgt *Signature of Witness.*

OATH TO BE TAKEN BY RECRUIT ON ATTESTATION.

I, Ronald Charles Colman do make Oath, that I will be faithful and bear true Allegiance to His Majesty King George the Fifth, His Heirs, and Successors, and that I will, as in duty bound, honestly and faithfully defend His Majesty, His Heirs, and Successors, in Person, Crown, and Dignity against all enemies, according to the conditions of my service.

CERTIFICATE OF MAGISTRATE OR ATTESTING OFFICER.

I William Harvey Anderson do hereby certify, that, in my presence, all the foregoing Questions were put to the Recruit, above named, that the Answers written opposite to them are those which he gave to me, and that he has made and signed the Declaration, and taken the oath at 59 Buckingham Gate on this 5th day of August 1914

W H Anderson 2/Lt *Signature of ~~Justice~~ of the Peace, Officer, or other person authorised to attest Recruits.*

If any alteration is required on this page of the Attestation, a Justice of the Peace should be requested to make it and initial the alteration under Section 80 (6), Army Act.

The Recruit should, if he require it, receive a copy of the Declaration on Army Form E. 501A.

* If so, the Recruit is to be asked the particulars of his former Service, and to produce, if possible, his Parchment Certificate of Discharge and Certificate of Character, which should be returned to him conspicuously endorsed in red ink, as follows, viz.—(Name) re-enlisted in the (Regiment) on the (Date)

† Here insert County. ‡ Here insert Corps.

JAN 27 1920

Fig 1 Private Ronald Colman - Attestation Form E.501 (WO 364/742)

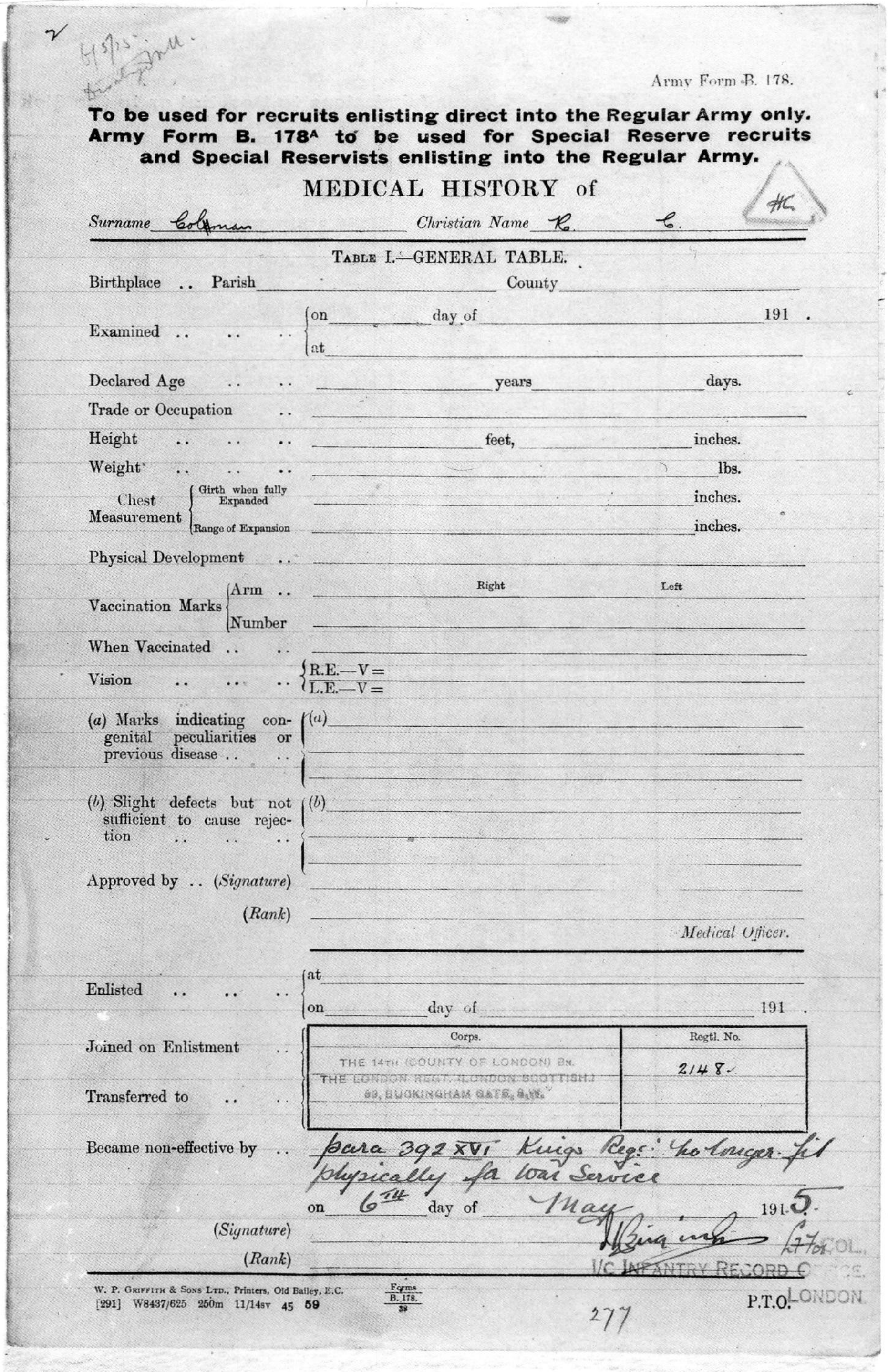

6/5/15. Discharged

Army Form B. 178.

To be used for recruits enlisting direct into the Regular Army only.
Army Form B. 178^A to be used for Special Reserve recruits and Special Reservists enlisting into the Regular Army.

MEDICAL HISTORY of

Surname Colman *Christian Name* R. C.

TABLE I.—GENERAL TABLE.

Birthplace .. Parish ______ County ______

Examined .. .. .. { on ______ day of ______ 191 . / at ______ }

Declared Age .. .. ______ years ______ days.

Trade or Occupation .. ______

Height .. .. .. ______ feet, ______ inches.

Weight .. .. .. ______ lbs.

Chest Measurement { Girth when fully Expanded ______ inches. / Range of Expansion ______ inches. }

Physical Development .. ______

Vaccination Marks { Arm .. Right ______ Left ______ / Number ______ }

When Vaccinated .. .. ______

Vision .. .. .. { R.E.—V= / L.E.—V= }

(*a*) Marks indicating congenital peculiarities or previous disease .. .. (*a*) ______

(*b*) Slight defects but not sufficient to cause rejection .. .. .. (*b*) ______

Approved by .. (*Signature*) ______

(*Rank*) ______ *Medical Officer.*

Enlisted .. .. .. { at ______ / on ______ day of ______ 191 . }

	Corps.	Regtl. No.
Joined on Enlistment ..	THE 14TH (COUNTY OF LONDON) BN. THE LONDON REGT. (LONDON SCOTTISH.) 59, BUCKINGHAM GATE, S.W.	2148
Transferred to ..		

Became non-effective by .. para 392 XVI Kings Regs: no longer fit physically for war Service

on 6th day of May 1915.

(*Signature*) H Bingham Lt Col.

(*Rank*) I/C INFANTRY RECORD OFFICE, LONDON

W. P. GRIFFITH & SONS LTD., Printers, Old Bailey, E.C. [291] W8437/625 250m 11/14sv 45 59

Forms B. 178. 39

277

P.T.O.

Fig 2 Private Ronald Colman - Medical History Form B.178 (WO 364/742)

Adm. to Pension 13-5-15

Rank *Private*

Regimental No. 2148

NAME *Ronald Charles Colman*

REGIMENT *London 3/14 Co. T.F.*

Date of Discharge 6-5-15

PENSION (First award) 18ᵈ 12 mos. cond⁸ & Board (Revised)

Pension District *War office*

Service

T.F. aub⁹.   9/12

Medals -

Character *Very Good*   Badges -

Grounds of Discharge *No longer physically fit for War Service*

Chelsea No. 26292-D.

Address:—
Strathrew - Muirton Place, Perth

Age on Discharge 24

Children's Allowance

Names of Children.	Dates of Birth of Children.

Foreign Service
India -
France and Belgium 1/2
Mediterranean Expeditionary Force -
Egypt -
South Africa -

Disability.   Fracture of Ankle (Rt)

In action near Ypres 31-10-14. Man states that when advancing a shell burst near him & he was thrown heavily in firing his right foot either by the fall or his foot being struck - There is considerable thickening of Rt ankle - There is also some tenderness & after walking any distance there is pain & lameness.
Medical Board :- Result of active service. Not permanent - at least 12 months. Prevents 1/4.

Casualty Form—Active Service   Army Form B. 103.

Regiment or Corps THE LONDON SCOTTISH. 14TH (C. OF L.) BATT. LOND. REG.

Regimental No. 2148   Rank Pt   Name R.C. Colman

Enlisted (a) 5/8/14   Terms of Service (a) 4 yrs   Service reckons from (a) 5. AUG 1914

Date of promotion to present rank   Date of appointment to lance rank   Numerical position on roll of N.C.Os.

Extended   Re-engaged   Qualification (b)

Date	From whom received	Record of promotions, reductions, transfers, casualties, etc. during active service, as reported on Army Form B. 213, Army Form A. 36, or other official documents. The authority to be quoted in each case.	Place	Date	Remarks taken from Army Form B. 213, Army Form A. 36, or other official documents
3.11.14	O.C. Abor 75 Amba	Admitted - Contusion R ankle	4 Lav 75 Amba	1.11.14	A36. No. 5924.
8-2-15	Ox 74 Hav Lon	Transferred to England		2/1/14 ?	
	3/14 Bn. London Regt. Disch⁹ᵈ	Para. 392 (XVI) King's Regs. not longer physically fit for War Service	Stamfd	21/14 6/15	Certified checked & brought up to date

Home   5.8.14   to   15-9-14 —   41 days
France   16.9.14   to   1-11-14 —   47
Home   2-11-14   to   6-5-15 —   186
2 Y 4

Lieut. Col.,
¹/o, Infantry Records,
3ᴿᴰ ÉCHELON G.H.Q.

for COL.

I/C INFANTRY RECORD OFFICE.
LONDON.

Fig 3 Private Ronald Colman - Royal Hospital, Chelsea, Pension Form (WO 364/742). Record cards such as this one are not commonly found on the service files. Colman's fracture eventually invalided him out of the army. His battalion, the London Scottish, was the first Territorial Battalion to go into action on the Western Front on 31 October 1914.

Fig 4 Private Ronald Colman - Casualty Form B.103 (WO 364/742)

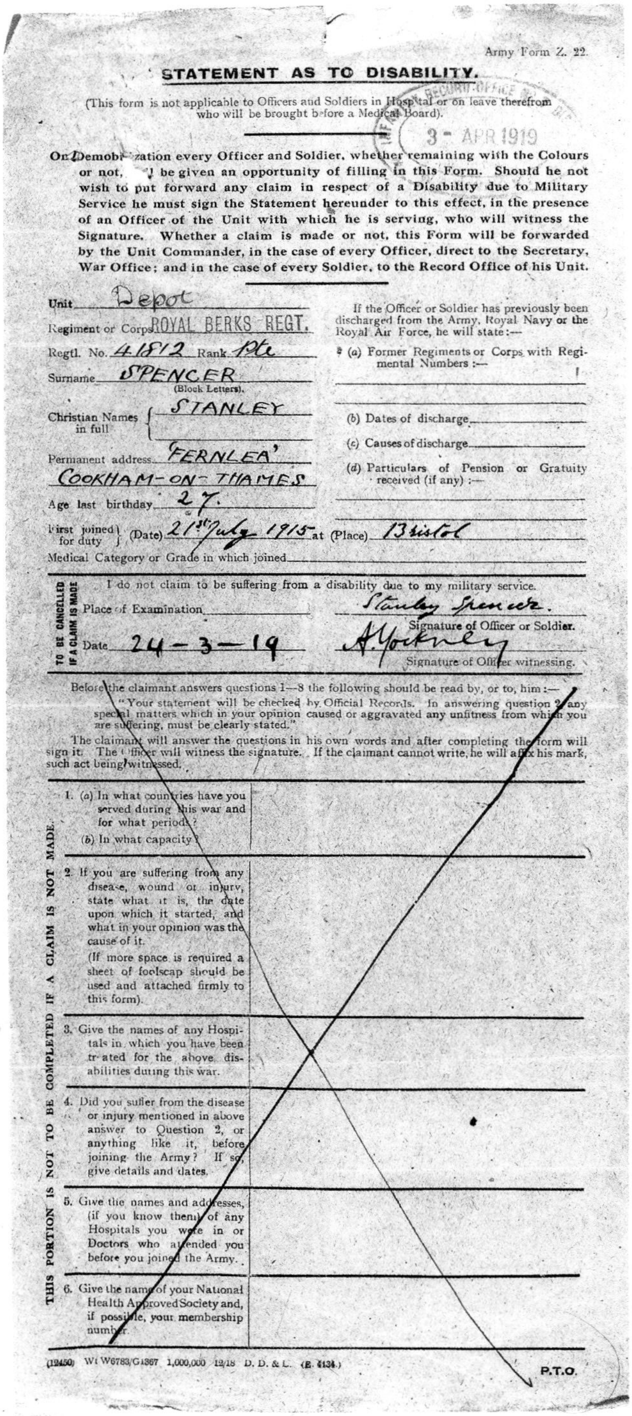

Army Form Z. 22.

STATEMENT AS TO DISABILITY.

(This form is not applicable to Officers and Soldiers in Hospital or on leave therefrom who will be brought before a Medical Board).

RECORD OFFICE ... 3 - APR 1919

On Demobilization every Officer and Soldier, whether remaining with the Colours or not, will be given an opportunity of filling in this Form. Should he not wish to put forward any claim in respect of a Disability due to Military Service he must sign the Statement hereunder to this effect, in the presence of an Officer of the Unit with which he is serving, who will witness the Signature. Whether a claim is made or not, this Form will be forwarded by the Unit Commander, in the case of every Officer, direct to the Secretary, War Office; and in the case of every Soldier, to the Record Office of his Unit.

Unit: Depot

Regiment or Corps: ROYAL BERKS REGT.

Regtl. No. 41812 Rank Pte

Surname (Block Letters): SPENCER

Christian Names in full: STANLEY

Permanent address: 'FERNLEA' COOKHAM-ON-THAMES

Age last birthday: 27.

First joined for duty (Date) 21st July 1915 at (Place) Bristol

Medical Category or Grade in which joined

If the Officer or Soldier has previously been discharged from the Army, Royal Navy or the Royal Air Force, he will state:—

(a) Former Regiments or Corps with Regimental Numbers :—

(b) Dates of discharge

(c) Causes of discharge

(d) Particulars of Pension or Gratuity received (if any) :—

TO BE CANCELLED IF A CLAIM IS MADE

I do not claim to be suffering from a disability due to my military service.

Place of Examination

Stanley Spencer. Signature of Officer or Soldier.

Date 24-3-19

A. Yockney Signature of Officer witnessing.

Before the claimant answers questions 1—8 the following should be read by, or to, him :—

"Your statement will be checked by Official Records. In answering question 2 any special matters which in your opinion caused or aggravated any unfitness from which you are suffering, must be clearly stated."

The claimant will answer the questions in his own words and after completing the form will sign it. The Officer will witness the signature. If the claimant cannot write, he will affix his mark, such act being witnessed.

THIS PORTION IS NOT TO BE COMPLETED IF A CLAIM IS NOT MADE.

1. (a) In what countries have you served during this war and for what periods? (b) In what capacity?
2. If you are suffering from any disease, wound or injury, state what it is, the date upon which it started, and what in your opinion was the cause of it. (If more space is required a sheet of foolscap should be used and attached firmly to this form).
3. Give the names of any Hospitals in which you have been treated for the above disabilities during this war.
4. Did you suffer from the disease or injury mentioned in above answer to Question 2, or anything like it, before joining the Army? If so, give details and dates.
5. Give the names and addresses, (if you know them) of any Hospitals you were in or Doctors who attended you before you joined the Army.
6. Give the name of your National Health Approved Society and, if possible, your membership number.

(12450) Wt W6783/G1367 1,000,000 12/18 D. D. & L. (E. 1134.)

P.T.O.

Fig 5 Private Stanley Spencer - Disability Statement Form Z.22 (WO 364/3886)

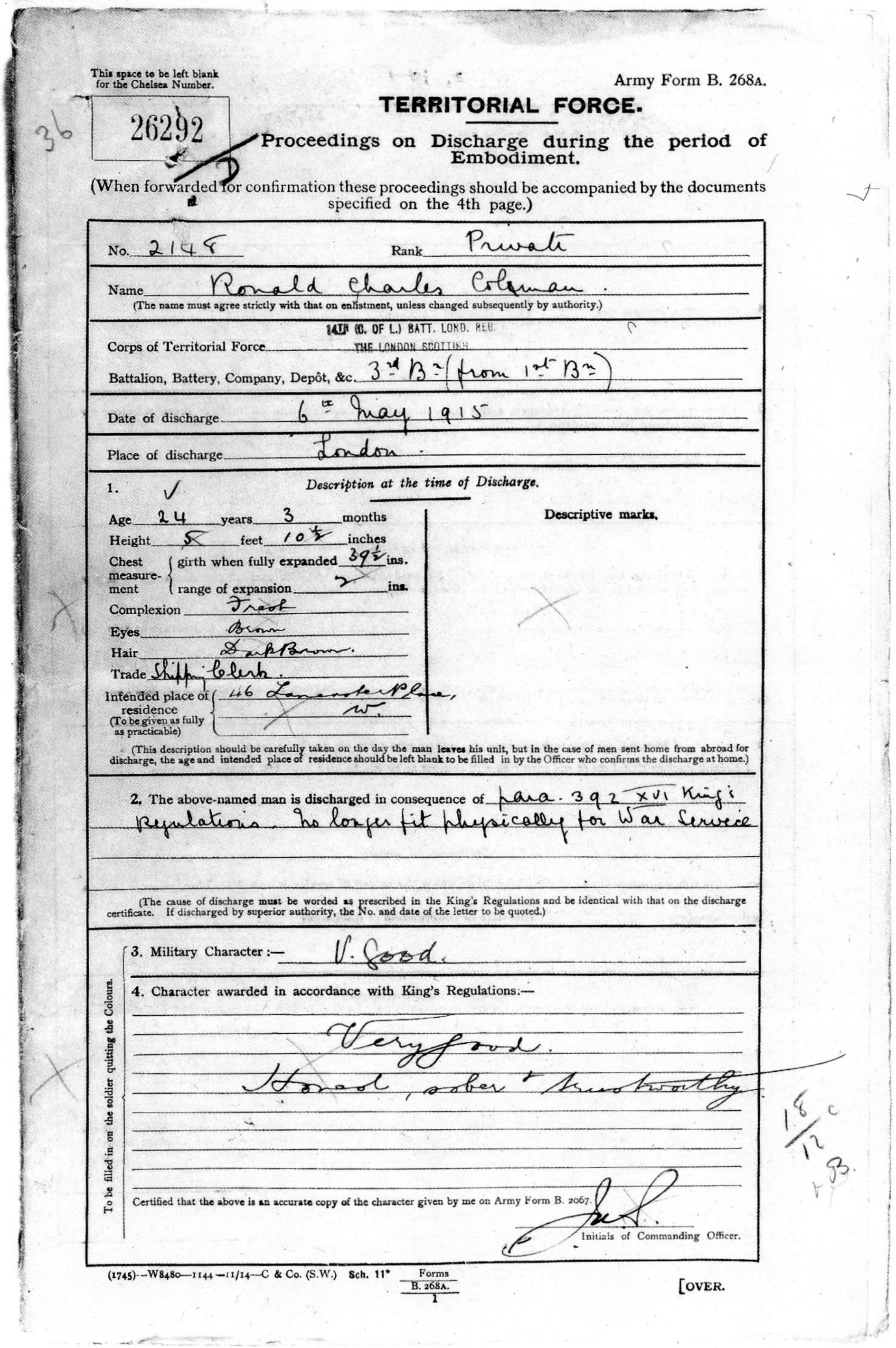

This space to be left blank
for the Chelsea Number.

Army Form B. 268A.

36

26292

TERRITORIAL FORCE.

Proceedings on Discharge during the period of
Embodiment.

(When forwarded for confirmation these proceedings should be accompanied by the documents
specified on the 4th page.)

No. 2148   Rank Private

Name Ronald Charles Colman .
(The name must agree strictly with that on enlistment, unless changed subsequently by authority.)

14th (C. OF L.) BATT. LOND. REG.
THE LONDON SCOTTISH

Corps of Territorial Force

Battalion, Battery, Company, Depôt, &c. 3rd Bn (from 1st Bn)

Date of discharge 6th May 1915

Place of discharge London .

1. ✓   *Description at the time of Discharge.*

Age 24 years 3 months

Height 5 feet 10½ inches

Chest { girth when fully expanded 39½ ins.
measure- { range of expansion 2 ins.
ment

Complexion Fresh

Eyes Brown

Hair Dark Brown .

Trade Shipp. Clerk .

Intended place of { 46 Lancaster Place,
residence { W .
(To be given as fully
as practicable)

Descriptive marks.

(This description should be carefully taken on the day the man leaves his unit, but in the case of men sent home from abroad for
discharge, the age and intended place of residence should be left blank to be filled in by the Officer who confirms the discharge at home.)

2. The above-named man is discharged in consequence of para. 392 XVI Kings
Regulations. No longer fit physically for War Service

(The cause of discharge **must** be worded as prescribed in the King's Regulations and be identical with that on the discharge
certificate. If discharged by superior authority, the No. and date of the letter to be quoted.)

3. Military Character :— V. Good.

4. Character awarded in accordance with King's Regulations :—

Very Good.

Honest, sober & trustworthy

To be filled in on the soldier quitting the Colours.

Certified that the above is an accurate copy of the character given by me on Army Form B. 2067.

Initials of Commanding Officer.

18 c
/12
43

(1745)—W8480—1144—11/14—C & Co. (S.W.) Sch. 11*   Forms
                                                      B. 268A.
                                                        1

[OVER.

Fig 6 Private Ronald Colman - Proceedings on Discharge Form B.268A (WO 364/742)

ROYAL HOSPITAL
5 - MAY. 1915
CHELSEA

List of Discharge Documents.

1. Proceedings on Discharge.
   Army Form B. 268A.

2. Agreement to serve outside the
   United Kingdom.
   Army Form E. 624.

3. Declaration on re-engagement.
   Army Form E, 611,

4. Army Form B, 97 (if any).

5. Declaration of change of name (if
   any).

6. Court of Enquiry on an injury (if
   any).
   Army Form A. 2,

7. Company or Field Conduct Sheet.
   Army Form B, 121 [or Army
   Form B, 122].

8. Copies of conviction by civil power
   (if any).

9. Medical History Sheet.
   Army Form B, 178,

10. Medical Report on invalid (if any),
    Army Form B, 179.

11. Attestation of Fraudulently En-
    listed men for corps in which they
    have not been held to serve (if
    any).

12. Descriptive Return,
    Army Form D, 400 where
    required—see Section 11
    on second page.

13. Active Service Casualty Form,
    Army Form B, 103,

14. Employment Sheet,
    Army Form A 2066,

INSTRUCTIONS as to the preparation, despatch and custody of Discharge Documents of Territorial Force N.C.Os. and men.

1. When a soldier of the Territorial Force is to be discharged during the period of embodiment, the attestation and the documents enclosed therein will be obtained from the Territorial Force Record Office and placed inside this form. Should any of the documents referred to in the margin be missing, an explanation of the deficiency, signed by the commanding Officer or Officer in charge Territorial Force Records, must be substituted for the missing documents. The Officer Commanding will also enclose any documents required to complete the list of discharge documents enumerated in the margin, The whole will then be placed in this form in the sequence there given,

2. When soldiers of the Territorial Force are discharged as medically unfit or with claims to pension, Army Form B. 268A will be sent, after confirmation of the discharge, with all the documents retained therein, to the Secretary, Royal Hospital, Chelsea,

3. In all other cases the discharge documents will be sent directly the discharge is carried out to the Officer in charge Territorial Force Records concerned.

4. Postage need not be paid and receipts are not required in the case of documents sent to Chelsea.

5. When the discharge documents of men not entitled to pension are sent to the Officer who will have final charge of them, they are to be accompanied by Army Form B. 279, and that Officer will, if they are found to be correct, sign and return Army Form B,279. Should any document be missing, he must at once apply for it.

6 The Officers having final charge of the discharge documents will arrange them according to Regimental numbers, and enter the names in the alphabetical index, Army Book No, 72.

MINISTRY OF PENSIONS
29 JAN
AWARD OFFICE
CHELSEA

Fig 7 Private Ronald Colman - Proceedings on Discharge Form B.268A, reverse (WO 364/742)

1.5 Common problems in tracing a particular individual

1.   **Which is my man?** As with all aspects of family history the more information you have before you start the easier it becomes. At the very minimum you will need to know which regiment and battalion he served with. The war medal cards (described in section 7.10) will normally give you his regiment, rank and number. The medal rolls will give you the battalion. Other information which may help you identify your man includes: date and place of birth, place of enlistment, wife's or father's name and address.

2.   **Where does my man's record start?** It can be difficult to work out where a record begins, especially if there are a number of men with the same forenames. Normally a man's document begins with his attestation paper. This is clearly marked Attestation Form. If your name is the very first or very last document on a film it is worth looking at the previous/next film to see whether his record continues on the new film.

3.   **I can't read the film.** Please ask the reading room staff for assistance. It is not possible to produce the original documents, as they are now too fragile to handle.

4.   **He isn't there!** If readers cannot locate a soldier's record, it may be because it has not been stored or filmed in the correct alphabetical order. Files discovered out of order after their letter series had been filmed were copied and placed at the end of the class. Alternatively, a file may have been out of order when filmed due to either a misspelling or misreading of a soldier's surname e.g. the record for a soldier with a first or second name Stanley may have been filed and subsequently filmed with soldiers of that surname, whilst a file of surname Allan may have been stored with the surname Allen. Double-barrelled surnames were sometimes wrongly filed. In addition, some soldiers did not record their first name on their service forms and instead used an initial, for instance H Davies, or a diminutive such as Bob or Bill. Until such time as a comprehensive nominal index is available, readers will need to think of possible alternatives if they are unsuccessful in their first attempt to locate a soldier. They should also bear in mind that there is a strong possibility that the record of service may not have survived.

You can ask the Ministry of Defence to do a search of the Burnt Documents for you. This will cost £20. Alternatively you should be able to construct something about your ancestor's career in the Army from other sources at the PRO or elsewhere, many of which are described below.

Don't forget that the Army may have recorded your ancestor under a slightly different surname from the one you know him by. For example, for Hayward, you should also check Heyward and Haywood/Heywood.

Chapter 2: Other sources at the Public Record Office

Having found your army service record, how can you discover more about what your ancestor did in the First World War? The *Battlefront* series of document study packs, produced by the Public Record Office, take an ordinary soldier's service record and show how it can be fitted into the context of other sources - war diaries, maps and photographs. *Battlefront: 1st July 1916. The first day of the Somme* (PRO Publications, 1996) includes the attestation papers of Private James Barnes of the 11th Battalion the East Lancashire Regiment, one of the 'Accrington Pals' who was wounded on the first day of the battle, and shows what happened to the rest of his unit and how this fitted into the overall strategic picture. *Battlefront: 6th November 1917. The fall of Passchendaele* (PRO Publications, 1997) uses a Canadian soldier who was born in Great Britain, Corporal William Rumford, and was wounded during the battle of Passchendaele.

2.1 War diaries

Although they rarely mention individual soldiers, war diaries are one of the most important sources to be found at the PRO for family historians trying to trace their ancestor's career in the British Army during the First World War. Almost all war diaries for the period of the First World War are in WO 95. A few war diaries were retained by the Ministry of Defence because they contained especially secret or confidential material. They have all recently been released and are now in WO 154. Maps which were previously kept with the diaries have mostly been extracted and are in WO 153. A typical page from a war diary is reproduced as fig 16.

As the name suggests a war diary is a day-by-day account of a unit's activity, whether on the front line or behind the trenches. The smallest unit which normally compiled a war diary was the battalion, which usually contained about a thousand officers and men. There are also war diaries for smaller specialist units, such as military hospitals.

It is unusual for war diaries to mention other ranks by name, although the death or wounding of an officer is usually mentioned. A report of a raid on the enemy may just record that 2nd Lt. Smith was killed, 4 other ranks (usually abbreviated to O.R.) were killed and 12 wounded. Each war diary however varies dramatically in the incidents reported. The amount of information recorded may depend on the enthusiasm of the junior officer who kept the diary. Naturally less coverage is given to periods when the battalion is resting or training behind the lines.

There are war diaries for British, Dominion, Indian and colonial forces serving in theatres of operations between 1914 and 1922, including the campaign in Russia and the various armies of occupation. Relatively few diaries survive for units which served solely in Britain. Diaries normally start when a unit formed or paraded in England before going overseas.

An index to war diaries arranged by battalion is at the front of the class list to WO 95, together with an index to Royal Field Artillery and Royal Garrison Artillery brigades and batteries. It is much harder to find war diaries for units which were neither infantry nor cavalry. In these cases you will normally need to know which Division, Corps or Army the unit was attached to. This information can be obtained from consulting the Orders of Battle in WO 95/5467-5487. The Orders of Battle list by theatre of war, month by month, the location of each unit and to which Division or Army they belonged.

2.2 Medical and disability records

Almost all medical records relating to the admission of men to casualty clearing stations or hospitals have been destroyed. The surviving sample of this material can be found in the record class MH 106. These surviving records illustrate some of the statistics relating to casualties which can found in the *History of the Great War based on Official Documents: Medical Services: Casualties and Medical Statistics of the Great War,* a copy of which can be found in the Microfilm Reading Room. Many of the admission books are Army Books 27a, *Admission and Discharge Book for Field Service.* These books provide name, rank, regiment or corps, company (if applicable), age, years of service, years of service with the expeditionary force, disease or injury, date of discharge or transfer and religion.

Other records in MH 106 include medical sheets for the Grenadier Guards Leicester Regiment, Royal Field Artillery and Royal Flying Corps.

The records in MH 106 are worth consulting if the individual you seek was wounded and you know where he was hospitalised or treated. Information about such treatment can sometimes be found on the Army Form B 103. Casualty Form- Active Service.

An example of an admission register, that for Craiglockhart Hospital in Edinburgh to where the war poet Siegried Sassoon was sent, can be seen in fig. 26 in Chapter 10.

Apart from the records in WO 364, which are very similar, a further collection of disability and widows' pension files can be found in PIN 26. As this record class derives from the Ministry of Pensions, it is possible to find files relating to Officers, Nurses and members of the Royal and Merchant Navies, as well as Army other ranks. Although there are over 20,000 individual files in PIN 26, those files less than 50 years old (ie those files which were still in use in 1947) are still closed.

A selection of widows' (and dependants') pension forms is in PIN 82. They survive for about one in twelve of claims. Each of the 183 pieces contains forms for about fifty servicemen arranged in surname order. Each form gives details of the serviceman's name, place of residence, particulars of service, and date and place of death or injury. The form also gives details of the pension awarded.

2.3 Published lists of names

Soldiers died in the Great War was first published in eighty volumes in 1921 and lists all the men who died between 1914 and 1919. It was reprinted in 1989 and copies may possibly be obtained from specialist military booksellers. A microfilm copy is in the Microfilm Reading Room and copies can be found in many other libraries and record offices. An index to the location of books for individual regiments is also available in the Microfilm Reading Room.

It is an essential tool to confirm the place and date of the death of an ancestor, although you will need to know the regiment he served with. These volumes will give you the battalion which, in turn, will make it easier to find the correct soldier's document or a war diary for the unit he served with but entries are not always wholly accurate. Each book contains the deaths for a particular regiment arranged in surname order by battalion. The entry for each man gives his place of birth, place of enlistment, service number, whether he died of wounds (abbreviated to DoW) or was killed in action (KiA) and approximately where this was. Any gallantry medals he may have won are also listed.

E.W. Bell (ed), *Soldiers killed on the First Day of the Somme* (1977) is, as the name suggests, a list of all the men known to have been killed on 1 July 1916. A copy of this book is available in the Microfilm Reading Room.

A National Roll of the Great War, 1914-1918 was published in 14 volumes for certain cities and towns in the years immediately after the end of the war. The *Roll* lists both men who survived as well as the fallen. It is thought that the publishers went into liquidation before the remaining volumes were published. Copies of most volumes are held by the Imperial War Museum and the complete set is held by the Society of Genealogists. The PRO does not have any copies. There are many errors with the entries and thus the *Roll* must be treated with caution. Further information is given in Norman Holding, *World War I Army Ancestry* (Federation of Family History Societies, Birmingham, 1997).

A number of companies published rolls of honour listing employees who had either served or who had been killed while serving in the British armed forces. Their survival rate is patchy. Where they survive, many of these rolls are to be found at the Imperial War Museum and local record offices. The PRO has several examples mainly for employees of railway companies, including the Midland Railway (RAIL 491/1259), the London, Brighton and South Coast Railway (RAIL 414/761), and the North Eastern Railway (RAIL 527/993).

2.4 Maps and photographs

Trench maps can give some idea of the terrain where your ancestor fought, although it should be remembered that for the most part they only show German trench formations.

To find the layout of British trenches you will need to consult the special 'secret' editions of maps, copies of which are in WO 297. The Imperial War Museum also has an extensive collection of trench maps. Part of a trench map is reproduced as fig 17.

Trench maps and aerial photographs have been reproduced in the two document packs published by the Public Record Office. *Battlefront: 1st July 1916. The first day of the Somme* (PRO Publications, 1996) and *Battlefront: 6th November 1917. The fall of Passchendaele* (PRO Publications, 1997). In the example below, taken from the Passchendaele pack, the capital letters **V**, **W**, **D** and **E** designate a large square. Each large square is subdivided into 30 smaller squares, numbered in sequence. Each smaller square should be mentally divided into four, the appropriate quarter being designated by **a**, **b**, **c**, or **d**. Each small square quarter has 1-10 northings and eastings taken from its south west corner. In the example below, **V.30** is the 30th small square in the larger **V** square. The **30** is in the middle of the square, surrounded by the imaginary sub squares **a**, **b**, **c** and **d** as shown in the diagram.

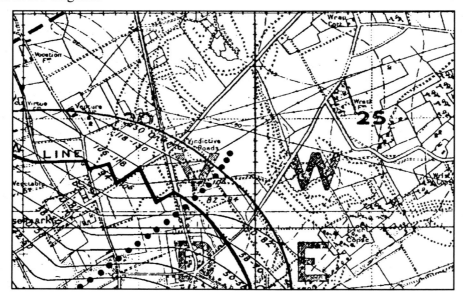

Most trench maps are in either WO 297 or WO 153. You will need to have a rough idea of the area of the Western Front you are interested in. Sometimes a war diary will give a map sheet reference either in the margin or in the body of the text. For more information about finding these maps you should consult the PRO leaflet, *How to Find and Use Trench Maps of World War I*, copies of which are available in both the Map and Large Document Reading Room and Research Enquiries Room. The key printed source is *Trench Maps a Collector's Guide* by Peter Chasseaud (1986).

The following classes of maps relating to First World War theatres of operations other than the Western Front are also available: WO 298 (Salonika), WO 300 (South West and

East Africa), WO 301 (Gallipoli), WO 302 (Mesopotamia), WO 303 (Palestine), WO 369 (Italy).

The Public Record Office holds surprisingly few photographs of the First World War; the vast majority of official photographs taken during the war are at the Imperial War Museum, including that on the front cover of this book. Some aerial photographs of the Western Front taken for reconnaissance purposes are in AIR 1. A small collection of photographs is also to be found in WO 316. Other small collections of mainly aerial photographs are in WO 317 (Gallipoli), WO 153 (Salonika), WO 319 (Palestine), and WO 323 (Italy).

2.5 Prisoners of war

The PRO holds no comprehensive lists of POWs on either side. It is thus almost impossible to find any information about an individual prisoner. The files in AIR 1/892/204/5/696-698 contain lists of British and Dominion prisoners of war held in Germany, Turkey and Switzerland in 1916. Of most interest are interviews with returned Prisoners of War, including officers and medical officers as well as other ranks, conducted by the Committee on the Treatment of British POWs, which are to be found in WO 161/95-101. Unfortunately there isn't an index to these records. Occasionally you might find correspondence about individual prisoners in the Foreign Office General Correspondence (FO 371), a card index to which is to be found in the Research Enquiries Room, although not all files that appear in the index have been selected for preservation. For further information on sources for Prisoners of War see PRO Leaflet 72, *Prisoners of War 1660-1919: Documents in the PRO*.

The International Committee of the Red Cross keeps records of all known POWs and internees of all nationalities for the First World War but is unable to deal with detailed genealogical enquiries.

Some printed monthly enquiry lists, issued during the war by the Enquiry for the Wounded and Missing Department of the British Red Cross and Order of St. John, listing the wounded and missing by regiment, are held by the Department of Printed Books at the Imperial War Museum.

2.6 Embarkation returns

Embarkation returns were compiled of units embarking for service overseas. Most of the surviving records appear to concern movement of troops across the Mediterranean Sea. They usually list officers (and on occasion their families), nurses and occasionally non-commissioned officers. Names of individual soldiers are not given. Lists for units leaving Britain or Europe are in WO 25/3533-3586. Lists for units returning to the United Kingdom or Europe are in WO 25/3696-3746.

2.7 Courts Martial Records

Registers of District Courts Martial for the period of the First World War are in WO 86/ 62-85. These registers give in tabulated form the name of the accused, his rank, regiment or corps, place of trial, charge and sentence. These courts only tried non-commissioned officer and other ranks. Registers of Field General Courts Martial, containing similar information but for more serious cases are in WO 213/2-26. WO 90/6-8 contain registers for General Courts Martial which took place abroad. They contain much the same information about each case as those in WO 86, but cover the trials of officers as well as other ranks. Proceedings for certain courts martial are in WO 71. They include records of trials of men shot for desertion, cowardice and other military offences. **At the time of writing (November 1997), the Ministry of Defence are carrying out a review of the cases where men were executed and therefore, many of these records are not available for consultation at the PRO. Please contact the PRO prior to an intended visit if you are interested in these records.**

If an individual was tried by court martial, the date and place where the trial took place,

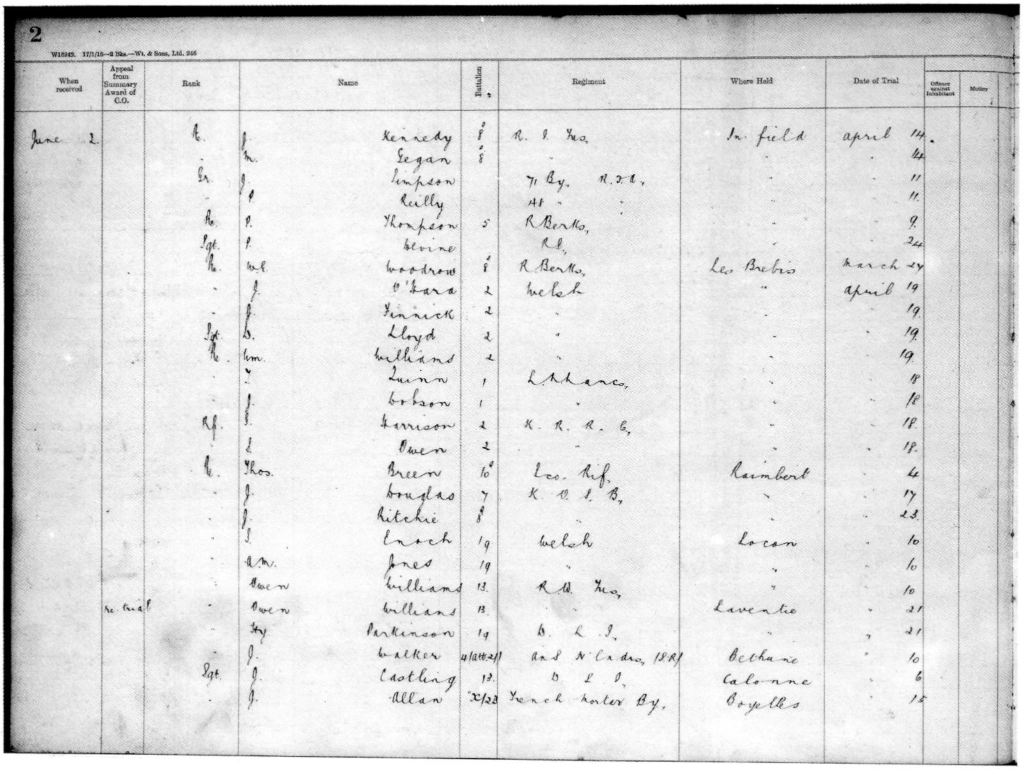

2

W18943. 17/1/16—2 Bks.—Wt. & Sons, Ltd. 246

When received	Appeal from Summary Award of C.O.	Rank	Name		Battalion	Regiment	Where Held	Date of Trial	Offence against Inhabitant	Mutiny
June 2		Pte.	J.	Kennedy	8	R. I. Fus.	In field	april 14		
		"	M.	Fegan	8	"	"	" 14		
		Gr.	J.	Simpson		71 By. R.F.A.	"	" 11		
		"	J.	Reilly		48 " "	"	" 11		
		Pte.	P.	Thompson	5	R. Berks.	"	" 9		
		Sgt.	P.	Devine		R.E.	"	" 24		
		Pte.	W.E.	Woodrow	8	R. Berks.	Les Brebis	march 24		
		"	J.	O'Hara	2	Welsh	"	april 19		
		"	J.	Finnick	2	"	"	" 19		
		Sgt.	D.	Lloyd	2	"	"	" 19		
		Pte.	Wm.	Williams	2	"	"	" 19		
		"	T.	Quinn	1	L.N.Lancs.	"	" 18		
		"	J.	Dobson	1	"	"	" 18		
		Rfn.	J.	Harrison	2	K. R. R. C.	"	" 18		
		"	E.	Owen	2	"	"	" 18		
		Pte.	Thos.	Breen	10	Lcs. Fus.	Raimbert	" 4		
		"	J.	Douglas	7	K. O. S. B.	"	" 17		
		"	J.	Ritchie	8	"	"	" 23		
		"	J.	Enoch	19	Welsh	Locon	" 10		
		"	A.M.	Jones	19	"	"	" 10		
		"	Owen	Williams	13.	R.W. Fus.	"	" 10		
	re-trial	"	Owen	Williams	13.	"	Laventie	" 21		
		"	Hy.	Parkinson	19	D. L. I.	"	" 21		
		"	J.	Walker	4/att. 2/1	and N. Lc. div. (S.R.)	Bethune	" 10		
		Sgt.	J.	Castling	13.	D. L. I.	Calonne	" 6		
		"	J.	Allan	X/23	Trench Mortar By.	Boyelles	" 15		

Fig 8 Register of Field General Courts Martial, June-July 1916 (WO 213/9)

together with the charge(s) and if found guilty, the sentence, should have been annotated on the individual's Casualty Form-Active Service, Army Form B 103 (see fig. 4). Details relating to a court martial may also have been added to the Regimental, Company or Field Conduct Sheet, Army Form B 121 or B122.

2250 Private Thomas Quinn, 1 Battalion Loyal North Lancs Regiment.

The record of service for Thomas Quinn can be found in WO 363/Q 30. The Army Form B 103, Casualty Form-Active Service records that in April 1916 he was tried by Field General Court Martial at Les Brebis on two charges; one of drunkenness and one of insubordination to a superior officer. Quinn was found guilty and sentenced to three months imprisonment with hard labour. Although no proceedings of the trial survive, the court martial was recorded at the Judge Advocate General's Office (JAG) in the Register of Field General Courts Martial for June-July 1916 (WO 213/9) (See fig. 8). The dates covered by each of these registers are the dates on which the information about the trial was received in the JAG office and not the date of the trial.

The court martial of Thomas Quinn was not his first encounter with the

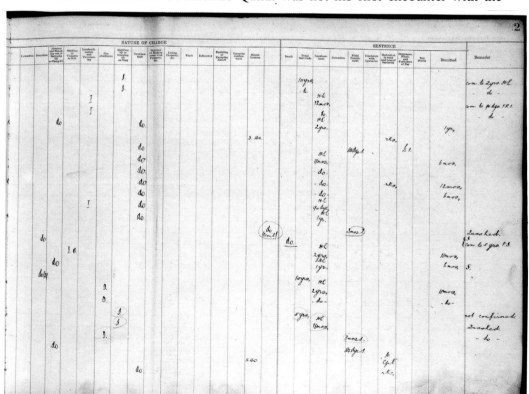

authorities. He had been previously punished on a number of occasions for minor offences. Thomas Quinn was killed in action in January 1918 whilst serving with 7 Battalion Loyal North Lancs.

It is possible to find details relating to the court martial of officers in their own individual records of service. Statistical information about the courts martial of men serving with Australian and Canadian forces between 1915 and 1919 are in WO 93/42-45.

Details of death sentences ordered by courts martial between 1914 and 1918 are in WO 93/49.

2.8 Miscellaneous records

French and Belgian death certificates for men who died outside the immediate war zones between 1914 and 1920 are in RG 35/45-69. They are arranged by initial letter of surname. WO 156 contains registers of baptisms for garrisons in the Dover and East Kent area for the period of the War.

Chapter 3: Officers' Records

3.1 Service records

Personnel records for those officers who saw service at any time during the First World War, are contained in two record classes which were opened to the public in February 1998. **However, if an officer saw service after 1922 his record will still be maintained by the Ministry of Defence.** For further details about post 1922 records contact the Ministry of Defence at CS (R) 2b, Bourne Avenue, Hayes, Middlesex, UB3 1RF.

Prior to the First World War, approximately 15,000 officers held a commission in the British Army. During the period of hostilities another 235,000 individuals were granted either temporary or permanent commissions in the British Army.

> Although approximately 250,000 individual files will have been in existence by the end of the First World War, only c.217,000 are being released. The difference is made up by those individuals who went on to serve after 1922, those who went on to serve in the RAF (records in AIR 76) and those files which have been destroyed.

Many of those individuals commissioned during the war served in the Royal Flying Corps. If their service terminated prior to the formation of the Royal Air Force (1 April 1918) their records may be found in either WO 339 or WO 374. If a member of the Royal Flying Corps served in the Royal Air Force, his record may be found in AIR 76, available on microfilm in the Microfilm Reading Room.

WO 339 contains the records of over 140,000 individuals and is arranged in what is called a "Long Number" order. In order to use this record class you need to obtain the "Long Number" by consulting WO 338/1-23, available in the Microfilm Reading Room. WO 338 is an alphabetical index which provides the relevant "Long Number" for an individual. Once you have obtained the "Long Number" for the record you seek, consult the WO 339 Class List and by looking for the "Long Number" on the right hand side of the page you should be able to identify the file and obtain the PRO reference which will be on the left hand side of the page.

Example of WO 338 index.

WO 338/17 Sa-Smith, George

Column Headings

Surname	Initial(s)	Regt/Corps	Long Number	Rank
Sassoon	S L	23	122091	2 Lt

Example of WO 339 Class List

Column Headings

PRO Group and Class and piece number	Surname and Initial(s)	Long Number
WO 339		
51440	Sassoon S L	122091

The second record class containing over 70,000 officers' records, WO 374, is arranged in alphabetical order. The dates contained in this class list are the dates of correspondence within a given file, rather than the dates of service.

Although the contents of the files vary, most contain some details relating to the unit(s) in which an individual served, medical details and in the case of those officers who were promoted from the ranks, their original attestation documents. If an officer was tried by court martial details relating to that trial can also be found. Records may also be found for those officers who were killed in action or died of wounds.

Apart from those forms which are common to other ranks and officers, two Army Forms specific to officers which may be encountered are:

Army Form B 201. *Application for Appointment to the Special Reserve of Officers.* Apart from providing the usual details about name, rank and unit etc, this form provides information about where an individual was educated and the name of the unit in which the individual wishes to serve.

Army Form MT 393. *Application for Appointment to a Temporary Commission in the Regular Army for the Period of The War.* This form is very similar to the one above but also asks the question whether an individual can ride ! (see fig. 9).

3.2 Published lists of officers

It is easy to confirm that an ancestor was an officer by checking the *Army Lists* which were published at monthly or quarterly intervals. Copies are to be found in the Research Enquiries Room. The Imperial War Museum, National Army Museum and certain other large libraries

138163/
1

NOTED ON CARDS

Form M.T. / M. 393

This Form is to be used for any candidate who is serving in the ranks of the New Armies, Special Reserve, or Territorial Force, and for any other candidate who is neither a cadet or ex-cadet of the Senior Division, Officers Training Corps, nor a member of a University. Form $\frac{M.T.}{392}$ should be used for an Officers Training Corps (Senior Division) or University candidate, who is not serving in the ranks.

APPLICATION FOR APPOINTMENT TO A TEMPORARY COMMISSION IN THE REGULAR ARMY FOR THE PERIOD OF THE WAR.

The candidate will complete the following particulars and obtain certificates below as to character and educational qualification.

1. Name in full	Surname.	Griffin
	Christian names.	William Harold
2. Date and place of birth.		1st October 1884. Salford. Lancs.
3. Whether married.		Widower (no family)
4. Whether of pure European descent.		Yes! ✓
5. Whether a British subject by birth or naturalization. (State which, and if by naturalization attach a certificate from the Home Office.)		British Birth
6. Nationality by birth of father (if naturalized, state date.)		British
7. Occupation of father.		Manager. (Engineering Works)
8. Permanent address of candidate.		103 West High St. Salford. Lancs.
9. Present address for correspondence.		19th (S) Royal Fusiliers.
10. School or Schools at which educated.		Salford Technical School.
11. Occupation or employment in civil life.		Municipal Accountant.
12. Whether able to ride.		Yes!
13. Whether now serving, or previously served, in any branch of His Majesty's Naval or Military Forces, or in the Officers Training Corps. If so, state :—		
(a) Regiment, Corps, or Contingent		19th (S) R.F.
(b) Date of appointment		1st May 1915
(c) If serving in the ranks state whether on an ordinary peace engagement or for the period of the war only		Period War.
(d) Rank		Private. (Signaller).
(e) Date of retirement, resignation or discharge		—
(f) Circumstances of retirement, resignation or discharge		—
14. Whether now serving, or previously served, in any other Government Department (Home, Indian, or Colonial). If so, give particulars.		No!
15. Whether an application for a commission has been previously made, if so, on what date and for what branch of the service.		No!

(7 30 32) G. D. 6684/2 20,000 11/15 H W V(P 660) H. 15/1275
W 16351—5516 20,000 1/16

Fig 9 Application for appointment to temporary commission for Lieutenant W Griffin - Army Form MT 393 (WO 339/63641).

also have sets. It can be time-consuming using some of the bulkier volumes, although they are all indexed.

The *Monthly Army Lists* contain lists of officers by regiment. Also included are lists of promotions, appointments and deaths of officers with date and reason. Of interest is the list of officers' war service which was published annually with the January issue, although information about service in the First World War is rather brief. An example is reproduced in Chapter 10.

Quarterly Army Lists include a graduation list, that is, lists of regular army officers by rank in seniority order, with dates of promotion and gallantry medals. Those published after 1918 include details of all extra-regimental appointments held by them during the First World War.

A number of books have been published listing the service of officers. Where the Office has copies they are listed below. Unless indicated, copies are available in the Research Enquiries Room. Please ask staff to show you where they are.

There is a separate volume (no. 81) of *Officers Died in the Great War* for officers, and it is available on the open shelves in the Microfilm Reading Room. It contains less information than the volumes for other ranks. For further information about these records see section 2.3.

A not dissimilar book is D.B. Jarvis and S.B. Jarvis, *The Cross of Sacrifice: Officers who died in the service of British, Indian and East African Regiments, 1914-1919* (Vol 1, 1993). This book, together with volume 2 (for the Royal Navy and Royal Air Force) and volume 3 (for Colonial and Dominion forces), is to be found in the Microfilm Reading Room. As well as giving details of how a man died it also indicates where he is commemorated.

Brief biographical descriptions, together with some photographs, of some officers who died during the war can be found in Marquis de Ruvigny, *The Roll of Honour: a biographical record of members of His Majesty's Naval and Military Forces who fell in the Great War* (2 vols, reprinted 1986).

Other brief biographical descriptions of officers can also be found in *A List of Commissioned Medical Officers of the Army, 1660-1960* (2 vols., 1925, 1968) and works such as Malcolm McGregor, *Officers of the Durham Light Infantry Vol 1 Regulars* (1989), and R.W. Walker, *To what end did they die: Officers who died at Gallipoli* (1980). Some regiments have published biographical lists of army officers who served in the First World War. A comprehensive collection is held by the Department of Printed Books at the Imperial War Museum.

General Staff officers and War Office staff (including civilian employees) are listed in the *War Office List* which was published by the War Office itself. The PRO only has copies for 1914, 1917 and 1918.

A list of officer prisoners of war was compiled by the military agents Cox and Co. in 1919. The *List of Officers taken prisoner in the various Theatres of War between August 1914 and November 1918* was reprinted in 1988.

Ledgers of payments to officers of disability pensions are in PMG 42. Other records relating to pensions for widows and payments to relatives of officers missing in action are in PMG 43-PMG 47. A small number of disability pension awards are in PIN 26.

Chapter 4: Records of other services

4.1 Royal Flying Corps

4.1.1 Officers

The records of service for officers of the Royal Flying Corps who went on to serve in the Royal Air Force after April 1918 and who relinquished their commissions before the mid 1920's can be found in the record class AIR 76. This record class which is available on microfilm in the Microfilm Reading Room, is in alphabetical order and can provide details relating to date and place of birth, date of first commission, units served in and decorations received.

4.1.2 Other Ranks

The records of service of those members of the Royal Flying Corps who were discharged before the Royal Air Force was formed on 1 April 1918, may be found in the 'Burnt' WO 363, or 'Unburnt' WO 364 record of service record classes.

4.2 Women

Women played a greater part in the First World War than in any previous conflict. Increasingly they took over clerical and other support roles in the armed forces freeing men to go to the front. Their nursing skills were also in great demand. Sadly though almost nothing survives in the Public Record Office. The Ministry of Defence at Hayes (see address under 1.1) holds personal files of the Women's Army Auxiliary Corps, some registers of Voluntary Aid Detachments and some records of Army nurses.

Perhaps the most useful record currently held in the Public Record Office is the microfiche card index of those women who were awarded campaign medals for service during the war and the associated medal rolls (WO 329). The medal rolls include those women who served in Queen Alexandra's Imperial Military Nursing Service (QAIMNS), Queen Alexandra's Imperial Military Nursing Service Reserve (QAIMNSR), Territorial Force Nursing Service (TFNS), Voluntary Aid Detachments (VAD), Women's Auxiliary Army Corps (WAAC) and the British and French Red Cross organisations.

Many nurses were awarded the Royal Red Cross (RRC) or Royal Red Cross 2nd Class

(ARRC). The award of these medals was announced in the *London Gazette* (see section 7.5). Recipients of the RRC and ARRC are noted in the *Army List.* A register of recipients of these awards can be found in WO 145.

An incomplete nominal roll for the Women's Army Auxiliary Corps is in WO 162/16. A list of women drivers employed by the Corps during the war is in WO 162/62 and recommendations for honours and awards are in WO 162/65.

Further information about nurses is given in PRO Information Leaflet no. 120, *Military nurses and nursing service: record sources in the Public Record Office.*

4.3 Nurses Records of Service

At the time of writing (November 1997) the Ministry of Defence have just started the preparatory work on these records, prior to transfer to the Public Record Office. The records to be transferred are for those individuals who served in Queen Alexandra's Imperial Military Nursing Service, Queen Alexandra's Imperial Military Nursing Service Reserve or Territorial Force Nursing Service and who joined the nursing services up to 1922 and who **did not** see service during the Second World War.

Chapter 5: Sources outside the Public Record Office

To build up a picture of a man's service in the Army during the First World War you may well need to use non-PRO records. Listed below are some ideas together with the places where you may find these records.

5.1 Newspapers

Newspapers are a seriously under-used resource for genealogy. This is largely because newspapers are rarely indexed and therefore it can be very time-consuming to go through issue after issue to find what you want. Between 1914 and 1918 newspapers were the only real way of finding out about the war. As a result they were heavily censored and so need to be treated with some caution. Even so it is possible to build up a good idea of the impact the war had nationally and on local communities.

Although the national newspapers carried lists of casualties and feted war heroes, most researchers will need to spend time looking at local papers. By the time of the war's outbreak almost every town and country district had one or more newspapers published at least weekly. They are listed in Jeremy Gibson, *Local Newspapers 1750-1920: a select location list* (Federation of Family History Societies, 1987). An almost complete set of newspapers is held at the British Newspaper Library, Colindale Ave, London NW9 5HE (0171 412 7353). Record offices and local history libraries may have newspapers for their areas.

Newspapers as mentioned above published casualty lists supplied by the War Office. Officers would appear in them about three weeks after their death and other ranks some six weeks after the event. Coupled with this were the small advertisements often placed by grieving relatives seeking information about men fallen or missing. On a more positive note, newspapers often carried letters which local men had sent back from France describing their life at the front. Local war heroes would be featured. Pictures were becoming more common in local newspapers and pictures of men in uniform were often carried.

5.2 Personal correspondence, diaries and mementoes

The volume of post exchanged during the First World War is estimated at 2000 million letters, cards and parcels from the front and 1600 million from home. Many of these letters have survived in family collections (see fig 15). Postal services between the front and home were good, as the authorities realised early on that letters from home were a real boost to morale. Photography had also become cheap enough so that for the first time a soldier could take a camera with him to France to record his life and that of his comrades in arms until private photography was formally prohibited in the summer of 1915. There were any number of keepsakes and souvenirs which could be bought or which were issued to people, from silver medals given to war wounded to patriotic handkerchiefs and embroidered postcards.

Where they survive mementoes should be treasured. They often tell us a great deal about the owner, whether it is a cheery note on a postcard, a photograph of a man standing uncomfortably in uniform, or most poignant of all, a last letter from a brother or son who was never to return. Norman Holding spends much time in *World War 1 Army Ancestry* and *More Sources of World War 1 Army Ancestry* interpreting sources which any family may have at home.

The major collections of personal documents relating to the First World War are held by the Department of Documents at the Imperial War Museum, Lambeth Rd, London SE1 6HZ (0171 416 5221), the Liddle Collection at the Brotherton Library, University of Leeds, Leeds, LS2 9JT (0113 233 5566), and the National Army Museum, Royal Hospital Road, London SW3 4HT (0171 730 0717 extn 2222). Similar collections held at regimental museums and other specialist military repositories are listed in *The Two World Wars. A Guide to Manuscript Collections in the United Kingdom* by S.L. Mayer and W.J. Koenig (Bowker, 1976). Up to date addresses of regimental museums are given in Terence Wise's *Guide to Military Museums* (1994). The Imperial War Museum Sound Archive (0171 416 5363) and the Liddle Collection also have large collections of tape recordings of men who served in the war.

5.3 War memorials

An everyday reminder of the sacrifice and the loss of the First World War which communities nationwide so deeply felt are the myriad war memorials to be found in every town and village. It can be difficult of course to find a memorial with your ancestor on. Men may be listed on the memorial where they lived, or where they were born, or indeed went to school. Occasionally memorials will also list men who served during the war as well as the fallen.

The information on memorials varies. They might just simply list names in alphabetical order. On the other hand they may also include regiment, as well as place and date of death. This information however should be treated with some caution as mistakes and omissions are not unknown.

A good introduction to the history and stories behind war memorials is Colin McIntyre, *Monuments of War: How to read a war memorial*. The Imperial War Museum has compiled a database of all known war memorials in Britain, although the database does not indicate on which memorials individuals may be found.

A number of companies produced memorial rolls of honour. They are to be found at the Department of Printed Books at the Imperial War Museum and many local record offices, as are similar rolls produced for individual villages or towns. A full list is given in Norman Holding, *The location of British Army records: A national directory of World War I sources*. A few company rolls, mainly for the larger railway companies, are at the PRO. Details are given above in section 2.3.

5.4 Commonwealth War Graves Commission

If you have an ancestor who died while serving in HM Forces, you will need to contact the Commonwealth War Graves Commission. The Commission is responsible for maintaining the cemeteries where men who served in British and Commonwealth forces are buried. It is a remarkable experience visiting a war cemetery with its row upon row of immaculately maintained gravestones. The Commission maintains a database which records where each man is buried or commemorated. They can also give you other information such as the regiment he served with and regimental number which may help you at the PRO. The Commission can also help with men who were missing believed dead and who thus have no known grave. The Menin Gate at Ypres is the memorial to the missing of Ypres. A similar monument to the missing of the Somme is at Thiepval in northern France. The best guide to all the battlefields and memorials on the Western Front is Rose E.B. Coombs, *Before Endeavours Fade: A Guide to the Battlefields of the First World War*.

The address of the Commonwealth War Graves Commission is 2 Marlow Rd, Maidenhead, Berks, SL6 7DX (01628 34221).

5.5 Birth, marriage and death records

Death certificates can be obtained from the Office of National Statistics (formerly the Office of Population Censuses and Surveys), Postal Application Section, Smedley Hydro, Trafalgar Rd, Birkdale, Southport, Merseyside, PR8 2HH or in person from the Family Record Centre (FRC). An example is reproduced as fig 14. Also at FRC are indexes to deaths which will give you a regiment as well as a date of death.

On a happier note, FRC also has registers of births of children to and marriages by soldiers both at home and abroad. Births and marriages may also be recorded in the soldier's documents in WO 363 and WO 364 where the documents themselves survive.

The ONS reading room in central London, formerly at St Catherine's House is now at: The Family Record Centre, 1 Myddelton Street, Islington, London EC1 1UX. The telephone number is 0181 392 5300.

Chapter 6: Service Records from other countries

Australia

Service records for men who fought in the Australian armed forces during the First World War can be obtained from the WW1 Personnel Records Section, Australian Archives, PO Box 117, Mitchell, ACT 2911, Australia. Enquiries about medals should be directed to Medals Section, CARO/SCMA, 360 St Kilda Rd, Melbourne, 3004, Australia. There is a charge of A\$15.00 per record which includes a photocopy of the man's service record. More information about the records is given on the Australian Archives Internet site. The URL for this is: **http://www.aa.gov.au.**'

Most records about a man's career in the Australian Imperial Force (AIF) are to be found at the Australian War Memorial. Of particular interest are the nominal and unit embarkation rolls which list everybody who left Australia to fight abroad. Roll of honour cards exist for those who died on active service. War diaries are also held by the AWM. Many of these records have been microfilmed and may be available in places other than Canberra. Further information may be obtained from the Manager - Information Services, Australian War Memorial, GPO Box 345, Canberra, ACT 2601, Australia.

Canada

Service records for Canadian forces are held by the Personnel Records Unit, Researcher Services Division, National Archives of Canada, 395 Wellington Street, Ottawa, Ontario K1A 0N3 (fax: (613) 947-8456). To enable the Unit to identify a service record, they require surname, forenames, and service number (or rank if officer). If you do not know the service number please supply date and place of birth or details of next of kin. (Other records, including thosed passed from the Directorate of History in the Department of Defence, are held by the National Archives of Canada, 395 Wellington St, Ottawa, K1A 0NA). More information about these records is given on the National Archives of Canada Internet site. The URL for this is: **http://www.archives.ca/www/PersonelRecords.html.**'

France

Service records for the 'Poilu', the nickname given to the ordinary French soldier of the period, are closed for 120 years. It is possible, however, for next of kin to get a limited extract from them. You will need to know the regiment an ancestor served with, together with his full name, and place and date of birth. Service records are held by the Service Historique de l'Armee de Terre, Vieux Fort, Chateau de Vincennes, 94304 Vincennes, France. A brief summary of the records available is given in Patrick Pontet, *Researches in France: A basic guide for family historians* (Andover, 1993). Copies are available from the Anglo-French Family History Society.

Germany

Service records for men who served in the Prussian Army during the First World War were destroyed or captured by the Russians during the Battle of Berlin in 1945. Many records are now coming back to Potsdam from the Russians which were once thought lost. The southern German states of Baden, Wurttemberg, and Bavaria, however, maintained their own armies. Their records survive and are available at the Landesarchiv in Stuttgart (for Baden and Wurttemberg) and the Kriegsarchiv in Munich (Bavaria).

New Zealand

Service records for New Zealand forces are held by Base Records, Ministry of Defence, Private Bag, Wellington, New Zealand. It should be remembered that many New Zealanders, especially those who had recently emigrated there, preferred to enlist in British regiments. The National Archives, PO Box 6148, Te Aro, Wellington hold many other records such as war diaries.

South Africa

Service records for South Africans are held by the Military Information Bureau, Archives Section, Private Bag X289, 0001 Pretoria, South Africa. The Bureau will do searches for family historians. Some other military records are held by the National Archives of South Africa, Private Bag X206, 0001 Pretoria.

United States

Records for the 'Doughboys', the American soldiers who fought in the First World War, are held by Military Personnel Records, National Personnel Records Center, 9700 Page Boulevard, St Louis, MO 63132 USA. Some 80% of these records were lost in a fire in 1973. However, the Center's holdings include other records of units and commands from which information can be abstracted concerning individual service. They also hold records of officers, as well as personnel records for the other American armed services roughly since 1912. They will only release information to next of kin. You will need to complete GSA Form R6-7231, copies of which are available from the Center.

War diaries and other records of the American Expeditionary Forces in France and elsewhere are held by the National Archives and Records Administration, Washington DC, 20408 USA from whom further information can be obtained.

Chapter 7: The Medal Records

Medals granted for service in the First World War fall into two distinct categories, those granted for gallantry or meritorious service and the campaign medals awarded to those men and women who saw operational service.

7.1 Awards for Gallantry and Meritorious Service

Many awards for gallantry and meritorious service were already in existence prior to the First World War.

The Victoria Cross (VC), open to all ranks from all three services, was instituted in 1856 as a reward for acts of outstanding bravery. The Distinguished Service Order (DSO) was instituted in 1886 as reward for those officers of the rank of Major or equivalent and below, who distinguished themselves on active service. The Distinguished Conduct Medal (DCM) was instituted in 1854 at the time of the Crimean War to recognise acts of gallantry or distinguished conduct by non-commissioned officers and men. By the late autumn of 1914 it became apparent that the existing awards needed to be supplemented by new ones.

The Military Cross (MC) was instituted in December 1914 (WO 32/5388) as a reward for gallantry for junior officers in the army (Captain and below) and Warrant Officers.

In early 1916, a further award was created to fill the gap which existed for those acts of gallantry which did not meet the standard required for the award of the DCM. The Military Medal (MM) instituted in March 1916 (WO 32/4960) was initially only awarded to non-commissioned officers and men but in 1917 the award was extended to women (WO 32/4959).

The Meritorious Service Medal (MSM) was instituted in 1845 as reward for soldiers above the rank of corporal. Prior to the institution of the DCM in 1854, it was possible for the MSM to be awarded for either gallantry or meritorious service. In either case the award was accompanied by an annuity. In October 1916 a Royal Warrant made changes to the eligibility of the award. These changes allowed awards to be made for gallantry not in face of the enemy or for valuable services in connection with the war to Warrant Officers, non-commissioned officers and men, but without an annuity.

For those individuals who were awarded the Distinguished Service Order or the Military Cross, it is possible to consult the *DSO and MC Gazette Books* in WO 389, rather than the *London Gazette*, in order to obtain a citation. WO 389/1-8 are arranged by gazette date and each individual volume is internally indexed. In many cases, the entries are annotated with the exact place and date on which the deed for which the award was granted was performed. (See fig.10). This information can be of great use when consulting the unit war diaries in

WO 95. WO 389/9-24 is an alphabetical list of those individuals who were awarded the Military Cross at any time prior to the Second World War and can provide the date on which the award was announced, the unit in which the individual was serving when the award was won and the date on which the individual received the award. (See fig. 11). WO 389 is on microfilm and is available in the Microfilm Reading Room.

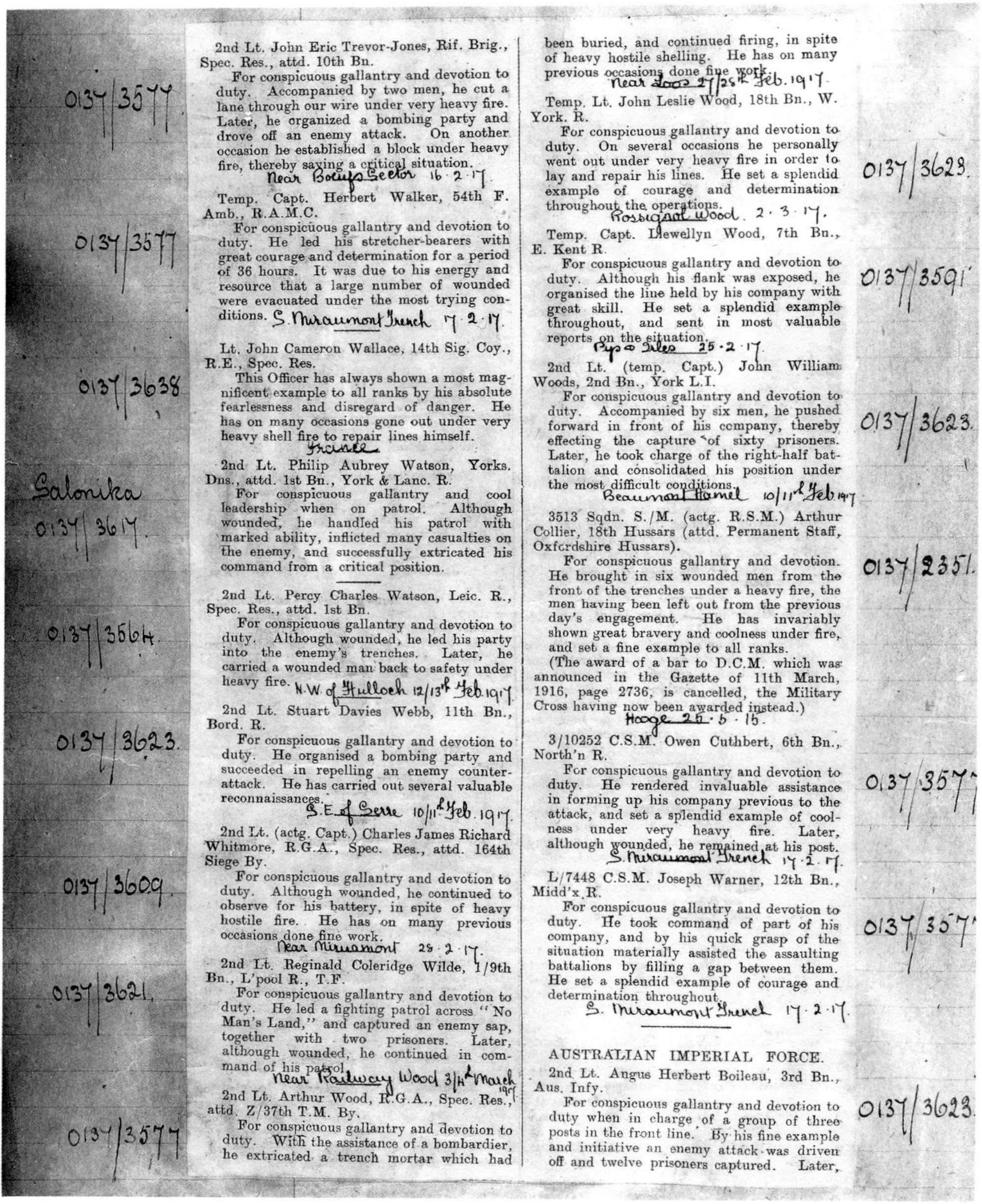

0137/3577

2nd Lt. John Eric Trevor-Jones, Rif. Brig., Spec. Res., attd. 10th Bn.

For conspicuous gallantry and devotion to duty. Accompanied by two men, he cut a lane through our wire under very heavy fire. Later, he organized a bombing party and drove off an enemy attack. On another occasion he established a block under heavy fire, thereby saving a critical situation.

Near Boeufs Sector 16·2·17.

0137/3577

Temp. Capt. Herbert Walker, 54th F. Amb., R.A.M.C.

For conspicuous gallantry and devotion to duty. He led his stretcher-bearers with great courage and determination for a period of 36 hours. It was due to his energy and resource that a large number of wounded were evacuated under the most trying conditions. S. Miraumont Trench 17·2·17.

0137/3638

Lt. John Cameron Wallace, 14th Sig. Coy., R.E., Spec. Res.

This Officer has always shown a most magnificent example to all ranks by his absolute fearlessness and disregard of danger. He has on many occasions gone out under very heavy shell fire to repair lines himself.

France

Salonika

0137/3617.

2nd Lt. Philip Aubrey Watson, Yorks. Dns., attd. 1st Bn., York & Lanc. R.

For conspicuous gallantry and cool leadership when on patrol. Although wounded, he handled his patrol with marked ability, inflicted many casualties on the enemy, and successfully extricated his command from a critical position.

0137/3564.

2nd Lt. Percy Charles Watson, Leic. R., Spec. Res., attd. 1st Bn.

For conspicuous gallantry and devotion to duty. Although wounded, he led his party into the enemy's trenches. Later, he carried a wounded man back to safety under heavy fire. N.W. of Hulloch 12/13th Feb. 1917.

0137/3623.

2nd Lt. Stuart Davies Webb, 11th Bn., Bord. R.

For conspicuous gallantry and devotion to duty. He organised a bombing party and succeeded in repelling an enemy counter-attack. He has carried out several valuable reconnaissances.

S.E. of Serre 10/11th Feb. 1917.

0137/3609.

2nd Lt. (actg. Capt.) Charles James Richard Whitmore, R.G.A., Spec. Res., attd. 164th Siege By.

For conspicuous gallantry and devotion to duty. Although wounded, he continued to observe for his battery, in spite of heavy hostile fire. He has on many previous occasions done fine work.

Near Miraumont 28·2·17.

0137/3621.

2nd Lt. Reginald Coleridge Wilde, 1/9th Bn., L'pool R., T.F.

For conspicuous gallantry and devotion to duty. He led a fighting patrol across "No Man's Land," and captured an enemy sap, together with two prisoners. Later, although wounded, he continued in command of his patrol.

Near Railway Wood 3/4th March 1917

0137/3577

2nd Lt. Arthur Wood, R.G.A., Spec. Res., attd. Z/37th T.M. By.

For conspicuous gallantry and devotion to duty. With the assistance of a bombardier, he extricated a trench mortar which had been buried, and continued firing, in spite of heavy hostile shelling. He has on many previous occasions done fine work.

Near Loos 27/28th Feb. 1917.

0137/3628.

Temp. Lt. John Leslie Wood, 18th Bn., W. York. R.

For conspicuous gallantry and devotion to duty. On several occasions he personally went out under very heavy fire in order to lay and repair his lines. He set a splendid example of courage and determination throughout the operations.

Rossignol Wood. 2·3·17.

0137/3591

Temp. Capt. Llewellyn Wood, 7th Bn., E. Kent R.

For conspicuous gallantry and devotion to duty. Although his flank was exposed, he organised the line held by his company with great skill. He set a splendid example throughout, and sent in most valuable reports on the situation.

Pys & Irles 25·2·17.

0137/3623.

2nd Lt. (temp. Capt.) John William Woods, 2nd Bn., York L.I.

For conspicuous gallantry and devotion to duty. Accompanied by six men, he pushed forward in front of his company, thereby effecting the capture of sixty prisoners. Later, he took charge of the right-half battalion and consolidated his position under the most difficult conditions.

Beaumont Hamel 10/11th Feb 1917

0137/2351.

3513 Sqdn. S./M. (actg. R.S.M.) Arthur Collier, 18th Hussars (attd. Permanent Staff, Oxfordshire Hussars).

For conspicuous gallantry and devotion. He brought in six wounded men from the front of the trenches under a heavy fire, the men having been left out from the previous day's engagement. He has invariably shown great bravery and coolness under fire, and set a fine example to all ranks.

(The award of a bar to D.C.M. which was announced in the Gazette of 11th March, 1916, page 2736, is cancelled, the Military Cross having now been awarded instead.)

Hooge 25·5·15.

0137/3577

3/10252 C.S.M. Owen Cuthbert, 6th Bn., North'n R.

For conspicuous gallantry and devotion to duty. He rendered invaluable assistance in forming up his company previous to the attack, and set a splendid example of coolness under very heavy fire. Later, although wounded, he remained at his post.

S. Miraumont Trench 17·2·17.

0137/3577

L/7448 C.S.M. Joseph Warner, 12th Bn., Midd'x R.

For conspicuous gallantry and devotion to duty. He took command of part of his company, and by his quick grasp of the situation materially assisted the assaulting battalions by filling a gap between them. He set a splendid example of courage and determination throughout.

S. Miraumont Trench 17·2·17.

AUSTRALIAN IMPERIAL FORCE.

0137/3623.

2nd Lt. Angus Herbert Boileau, 3rd Bn., Aus. Infy.

For conspicuous gallantry and devotion to duty when in charge of a group of three posts in the front line. By his fine example and initiative an enemy attack was driven off and twelve prisoners captured. Later,

Fig 10 Military Cross Gazette Book (WO 389/3)

```
┌──────────────────────────────────────────────────────────────┐
│                      Military Cross                            │
│                                                                │
│   Name            Wood            Arthur                       │
│   Rank            2 Lt                                         │
│   Regt/Corps      RGA (SR) att Z/37 TM Bty                     │
│   Gazetted to MC  17.4.17         Decorated      22.10.19      │
│   1st Bar to MC                   Decorated                    │
│   2nd Bar to MC                   Decorated                    │
│   Date of Death                                                │
│                                                                │
│                                                                │
└──────────────────────────────────────────────────────────────┘
```

Fig 11 Military Cross Name Index (WO 389/24)

7.2 Orders of Chivalry

Excluding the awards for gallantry mentioned above, it was also possible for Warrant Officers and above to be appointed to one of the Orders of Chivalry as a reward for meritorious service. The most frequent orders to which Warrant Officers or Officers could be appointed included The Most Honourable Order of The Bath, established in 1725, The Most Distinguished Order of St Michael and St George, established in 1818 and The Most Excellent Order of The British Empire, established by King George V in 1917.

7.3 Mentioned in Despatches

Mentions in Despatches (MiD) were in existence long before the First World War. The original purpose of the MiD was to bring to the notice of a higher authority the services of deserving officers only. However, by the time of the Boer War (1899-1902) both officers and men were being mentioned.

Prior to 1902 not all despatches were published in the *London Gazette*. At that time it was decided by the Interdepartmental Rewards Committee that only publication in the *London Gazette* would constitute a Mention in Despatches.

During the First World War approximately 2.3% of the total men under arms were Mentioned in Despatches. Due to the large number of MiDs being awarded, some people felt that the award was being devalued. It was decided in 1919 that a special certificate would be given to all those personnel who had been mentioned. In 1920 it was decided that a bronze oak leaf emblem should be worn on the ribbon of the Victory Medal to signify that the wearer had been Mentioned in Despatches. Only one emblem could be worn however many times the individual had been mentioned.

In all except a few cases, any award granted for gallantry or meritorious service, an appointment to one of the Orders of Chivalry, or a Mention in Despatches would be announced in the *London Gazette*.

7.4 Citations

Citations give brief details describing the act(s) for which a gallantry award was granted. These citations were usually written using material taken from the Army Form W3121 "Recommendation for Awards" completed by the officer who was recommending the individual for an award. Except in extremely rare cases, the vast majority of the Army Form W3121s for awards granted during the First World War were destroyed by enemy action in 1940.

Citations usually accompanied the announcement of awards in the *London Gazette*. However, not all announcements were accompanied by a citation. Apart from the Victoria Cross, which always had a citation, many of those awards announced in the New Year or Birthday Honours lists did not. At other times of the year most awards were accompanied by citations, either in the *London Gazette* announcing the award or in a later edition. Apart from the first seventy seven Military Medals awarded to nurses, there were no published citations for the Military Medal, Meritorious Service Medal or for Mentions in Despatches. However, it is sometimes possible to find details relating to awards of the MM and MSM in the Unit War Diaries in WO 95.

It is possible to find citations for the following awards in the *London Gazette*: The Victoria Cross, Distinguished Service Order, Military Cross and Distinguished Conduct Medal.

7.5 The *London Gazette*

The *London Gazette*, founded in 1665, is the official paper of the government, containing acts of state, proclamations and appointments to offices under the crown. All military appointments and announcements relating to awards for gallantry and meritorious service or Mentions in Despatches are published in the *London Gazette*. The paper is published periodically throughout each month of the year. The page numbering is sequential from the beginning of the year to the end. At the end of each quarter (March, June, September and December), half (June and December) or end (December) of the year, indexes are published which list the subjects and names of individuals which have appeared in the *London Gazette* during a given period. The *London Gazette* is in the class ZJ 1. Each piece of the class is either a bound volume containing the *London Gazette* for one or sometimes two months or an index volume.

In order to find the particular entry for an individual, you need to have certain information which will enable you to find the correct edition. It will help if you have any of the following; Name, Rank and Unit, Type of Award and the approximate date.

The indexes for the *London Gazette* are available in the Microfilm Reading Room and you should consult these volumes first. Each year from 1914-1921 is split into quarters. In each quarter, the different awards are listed alphabetically, for example the Distinguished Conduct Medal appears before the Military Cross. Under each award there are lists of names in alphabetical order of those individuals who have been granted that award. Alongside each name is a number; this is a page number for a particular edition of the *London Gazette*. In order to identify which piece of the ZJ 1 class you need to order, you should consult the ZJ 1 class list. After finding the particular year, find the month which encompasses the page number of the individual you are interested in. The page numbers are alongside the names of the months. The piece number of the *London Gazette* you should order is in the left hand column. An example illustrating how to use the *London Gazette* is given below.

If you are unable to find the name of an individual who received the DCM, MM or MSM in the indexes of the *London Gazette*, you may wish to consult the Microfiche Card Indexes for those awards in the Microfilm Reading Room. These indexes provide the same information as the *London Gazette* indexes and the information should be used in the same way.

To find the *London Gazette* entry for those individuals who were Mentioned in Despatches you should to consult the alphabetical Microfiche Card Indexes in the Microfilm Reading Room. There are three different indexes and it may be necessary to consult all 3. As with the indexes for the DCM, MM and MSM, once you have found the details of the individual you are interested in, you will need to use the Class List for the *London Gazette* to find the correct edition containing the announcement of the MiD.

For details about all of the British Gallantry awards mentioned in this book, together with details about Mentioned in Despatches please refer to Abbott, P E and Tamplin, J M A, *British Gallantry Awards* (1981). A copy of this book is available in the Research Enquiries Room.

Using the *London Gazette* - an example

It is known that Sgt G Buse of the 14 Welch Regiment was awarded a Military Medal in August 1916. In order to find the announcement of his award you need to consult the *London Gazette* indexes for the third quarter of 1916 (ZJ 1/634). On page 28 in the State Intelligence section, under the title of Military Medal, the name of Sgt G Buse is found with the page number 8654. Taking this number to the *London Gazette* class list, page 8654 is to be found in the *London Gazette* of September 1916. To order this particular volume on the computer the reference you require is in the left hand column, in this case ZJ 1/636. The full entry merely states that the King has awarded the Military Medal "for bravery in the field" to the undermentioned ladies and non-commissioned officers and men, followed by a list of the two groups in alphabetical order, including "17834 Sjt. G. Buse, Welch R".

7.6 Campaign Medals and The Silver War Badge

Five different campaign medals were awarded for service during the First World War and apart from exceptional cases, the maximum number of medals which could be awarded to one man or woman was three. The medals were; the 1914 Star, the 1914/15 Star, the British War Medal 1914-1920, the Victory Medal 1914-1919 and the Territorial Force War Medal 1914-1919.

The 1914 Star, authorised in 1917, was awarded to servicemen and women and some civilians who saw service in France and Belgium between 5 August and 22 November 1914. In 1919 a bar with the inscription "5th Aug-22nd Nov.1914" was sanctioned. Only those personnel who had actually been under fire during the above specified period were eligible. The 1914 Star was not awarded on its own; it should always be accompanied by the British War and Victory Medals.

The 1914/15 Star, authorised in 1918, was awarded to servicemen and women and civilians who saw service in France, Belgium, the Dardanelles, East and West Africa and other small theatres of war between 5 August 1914 and 31 December 1915. The 1914/15 Star was not awarded to those personnel who had already qualified for the 1914 Star. The 1914/15 Star was not awarded on its own; as with the 1914 Star, it should always be accompanied by the British War and Victory Medals.

The British War Medal 1914-1920, authorised in 1919, was awarded to servicemen and women and civilians. Qualification for the medal varied slightly depending on which service the individual was in. The basic requirement for Army personnel was that they either entered a theatre of war or rendered approved service overseas between 5 August 1914 and 11 November 1918. Service in Russia between 1919 and 1920 also qualified for the award. The British War Medal could be awarded on its own. Many men who only served in India during the First World War received a single British War Medal.

The Victory Medal 1914-1919 was also authorised in 1919 and awarded to those military and civilian personnel who served on the establishment of a unit in an operational theatre. The Victory Medal could not be awarded on its own but should always be accompanied by at least the British War Medal.

The Territorial Force War Medal 1914-1919 was awarded to members of the Territorial Force only. To qualify for the award the individual had to be a member of the Territorial Force on or prior to 30 September 1914, and to have served in an operational theatre outside the United Kingdom between 5 August 1914 and 11 November 1918. Those men who were awarded the 1914 or 1914/15 Star could not receive the Territorial Force War Medal.

The Silver War Badge was authorised in September 1916. The badge was awarded to those officers and men who had retired or been discharged due to sickness or wounds caused by war service, either at home or abroad any time after 4 August 1914.

Some of the campaign medals awarded for service during the First World War were known by unofficial names or nicknames. The 1914 Star is sometimes called the "Mons Star". A group of medals awarded to an individual which consisted of either of the Stars and the British War and Victory medals, was sometimes known as "Pip, Squeak and Wilfred". If the British War and Victory medals are on their own, they were sometimes known as "Mutt and Jeff".

The medal rolls for the 1914 Star, 1914/15 Star, British War Medal 1914-1920, Victory Medal 1914-1919, Territorial Force War Medal 1914-1919 and the Silver War Badge are in the class WO 329.

7.7 How to use the First World War Medal Rolls (WO 329)

To search the medal rolls in WO 329, you need to consult the Medal Index Cards (MIC) in the class WO 372 first. These cards are on microfiche and are held in the Microfilm Reading Room. An example is given in section 7.10 below.

WO 372 is an alphabetical list of those individuals who qualified for any of the following campaign medals; 1914 Star, 1914/15 Star, British War Medal 1914-1920, Victory Medal 1914-1919, Territorial Force War Medal 1914-1919 and/or were awarded a Silver War Badge.

The MICs are in alphabetical sequence and Regimental Order of Precedence. Names of individuals are usually listed in the following format.

Jones J
Jones James
Jones John
Jones Julius
Jones James A
Jones John A

Jones Julius A
Jones James B
Jones John B
Jones Julius B
Jones James A B
Jones John A B

This sequence of surname, followed by single initial, followed by single forename, followed by forename and initial(s), is used throughout the Medal Index Cards. Each sequence of names is also listed in Regimental Order of Precedence, whereby those men who served in the most senior regiment in the army appear first and men from the second most senior and subsequent regiments, appear in a specific order (see 7.9).

On each Medal Index Card the following information is given: Surname; First Forename, Name or initial and subsequent initials; Rank; Regiment; Service Number; the Medals to which the individual was entitled and the Army Medal Office medal roll references for these medals; the name or number of the first operational theatre in which the individual first served and the date when the individual first entered that theatre. Usually the name of the theatre is given in full but in some cases just a number and/or letter is given. There were 26 different operational theatres, details of which can be found in 7.8. The Army Medal Office references usually appear in the form of an alphanumerical code, the last part of which is the page number on which the name of the individual appears.

The MICs were filmed onto sheets of microfiche and each sheet contains 360 MICs. When the MICs were filmed they were laid out in a specific pattern. An example of the way in which the microfiche is laid out can be found in 7.10.

In order to obtain the correct WO 329 references for the medal rolls and Silver War Badge roll, the sequence to use is as follows. An example is given in 7.10.

- Find the sheet of microfiche which includes the surname of the individual you are interested in.
- Find the name of the individual on the MIC.
- Write down the details of Army Medal Office reference numbers, which are noted alongside the names of the medals an individual was awarded.
- Change the Army Medal Office references into WO 329 references using WO 329/1 key, which is available in the Microfilm Reading Room, as a copied bound volume.
- Order the WO 329 volume you require on one of the Computer Terminals in the Research Enquiries Room.

It is possible to obtain photocopies of both the Medal Index Cards and the Medal Rolls. Please speak to the staff in the Microfilm Reading Room .

7.8 Operational Theatres of War 1914-1920 - alphanumeric codes

The alphanumeric codes for each theatre of war, e.g. 1a relating to service in France and Belgium in the Western European theatre of war, are also used in the service records. For those men who first saw operational service before 31/12/1915 and therefore received a 1914 Star or 1914/15 Star, as well as the British War and Victory Medals, the numerical codes used differ slightly from those used for men who only saw their first operational service from 1/1/1916 onwards.

Pre 31/12/1915   Post 1/1/1916

1   1   Western Europe
    a   France and Belgium
    b   Italy

2   2   Balkans
    a   Greek Macedonia, Serbia, Bulgaria and European Turkey
    b   Gallipoli (Dardanelles)

  3   Russia (4/5 August 1914-1/2 July 1920)

3   4   Egypt
    a   4/5 November 1914-18/19 March 1916
    b   18/19 March 1916-31 October/1 November 1918

4   5   Africa
    a   East Africa, Nyasaland and Northern Rhodesia
    b   South West Africa
    c   Cameroon
    d   Nigeria
    e   Togoland

5   6   Asia
    a   Hedjaz
    b   Mesopotamia
    c   Persia
    d   Trans Caspia
    e   South West Arabia
    f   Aden
    g   Frontier regions of India
    h   Tsing-Tau

6   7   Australasia
    a   New Britain
    b   New Ireland
    c   Kaiser Wilhelmland
    d   Admiralty Islands
    e   Nauru
    f   German Samoa

For more details relating to these operational theatres, see, Joslin, EC, Litherland, AR and Simpkin, BT, *British Battles and Medals*, Spink, (1988), pp 230-231.

7.9 Regimental Order of Precedence

For a comprehensive list of all regiments in order of precedence, see *British Battles and Medals* (above).

1 Life Guards
2 Life Guards
Royal Horse Guards
Household Battalion
Royal Horse Artillery
1 Dragoon Guards
2 Dragoon Guards
3 Dragoon Guards
4 Dragoon Guards
5 Dragoon Guards
6 Dragoon Guards
7 Dragoon Guards
1 Dragoons
2 Dragoons
6 Dragoons
5 Lancers
9 Lancers
12 Lancers
16 Lancers
21 Lancers
The Yeomanry Regiments
Royal Artillery
Royal Field Artillery
Royal Garrison Artillery
Royal Engineers
Royal Signals
Grenadier Guards
Coldstream Guards
Scots Guards
Irish Guards
Welsh Guards
Royal Scots
Queen's Regt (Royal West Surrey)
Buffs (East Kent)
King's Own Regt
Northumberland Fusiliers
Royal Warwickshire Regt
The Royal Fusiliers
The King's (Liverpool Regt)

Norfolk Regt
Lincolnshire Regt
Devon Regt
Suffolk Regt
Somerset Light Infantry
Prince of Wales's Own (West Yorkshire Regt)
East Yorkshire Regt
Bedford Regt
Leicester Regt
Royal Irish Regt
Yorkshire Regt (Green Howards)
Lancashire Fusiliers
Royal Scots Fusiliers
Cheshire Regt
Royal Welch Fusiliers
South Wales Borderers
King's Own Scottish Borderers
Cameronians (Scottish Rifles)
Royal Inniskilling Fusiliers
Gloucester Regt
Worcester Regt
East Lancashire Regt
East Surrey Regt
Duke of Cornwall's Light Infantry
Duke of Wellington's (West Riding Regt)
Border Regt
Royal Sussex Regt
Hampshire Regt
South Staffordshire Regt
Dorset Regt
Prince of Wales's Volunteers (South Lancashire Regt)
Welsh Regt
Black Watch (Royal Highlanders)
Oxfordshire and Buckinghamshire Light Infantry

Essex Regt
Sherwood Foresters (Notts and Derby Regt)
Loyal North Lancashire Regt
Northamptonshire Regt
Princess Charlotte of Wales's (Royal Berkshire Regt)
Queen's Own (Royal West Kent Regt)
King's Own Yorkshire Light Infantry
Shropshire Light Infantry
Duke of Cambridge's Own (Middlesex Regt)
King's Royal Rifle Corps
Duke of Edinburgh's (Wiltshire Regt)
Manchester Regt
Prince of Wales's (North Staffordshire Regt)
York and Lancaster Regt
Durham Light Infantry
Highland Light Infantry
Seaforth Highlanders
Gordon Highlanders
Queen's Own Cameron Highlanders
Royal Irish Rifles
Princess Victoria's (Royal Irish Fusiliers)
Connaught Rangers

Princess Louise's (Argyll and Sutherland Highlanders)
Prince of Wales's Leinster Regt
Royal Munster Fusiliers
Royal Dublin Fusiliers
Rifle Brigade
Machine Gun Corps
Royal Tank Corps
Labour Corps
Royal Army Chaplains Department
Royal Army Service Corps
Royal Army Medical Corps
Royal Army Ordnance Corps
Royal Army Veterinary Corps
Honourable Artillery Company
The Territorial Force units
Monmouthshire Regt
Cambridgeshire Regt
London Regt
Inns of Courts Officers Training Corps
Hertfordshire Regt
Herefordshire Regt
Northern Cyclist Bttn
Highland Cyclist Bttn
Kent Cyclist Bttn
Huntingdon Cyclist Bttn

7.10 WO 372 Medal Index Card Microfiche Layout

On each sheet of microfiche there are 360 separate index cards. The first card is in the top left hand corner (1), the last card in the bottom right hand corner (360). The cards have been filed in alphabetical order and in regimental order of precedence, given in section 7.9.

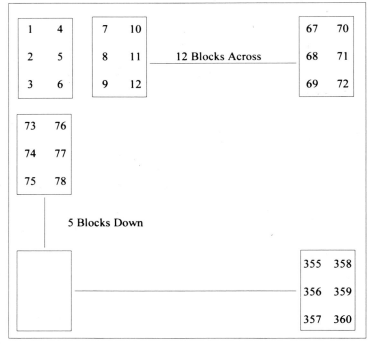

WO 372 Medal Index Card layout

Name.	Corps.	Rank.	Regtl No.
	14 LOND. R	*Pte*	*2148*
COLMAN			
Ronald C			

Medal.	Roll.	Page.	Remarks.
VICTORY	*TP14/101B*	*13*	*Disc 4.5.15*
BRITISH	*-do-*	*-do-*	*24/1/72*
14 STAR	*TP 5*	*17*	
Clasp 45122 CL & R in 461/c 18-	*1-22*		
SaB List TP/1283			
Theatre of War first served in			
Date of entry therein	*15. 9. 14*		

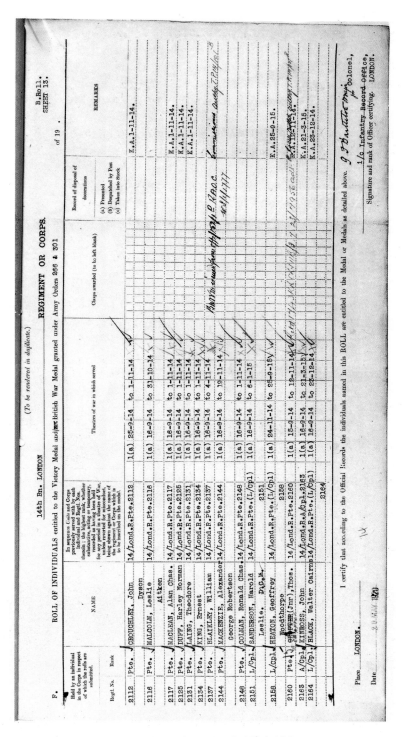

Fig 12 Medal Roll entry for Ronald Colman (WO 329/1928)

This example of the Medal Index card for Ronald C Colman shows that he served as a private with the 14th Battalion of the London Regiment and was discharged in May 1915. He was awarded the Victory Medal, the British War Medal and the 1914 Star and this is recorded on the Medal Rolls under the references TP 14/101B page 13 and TP 5 page 17, which have to be converted into WO 329 references (see below). He was also awarded clasps and roses (for the 1914 Star). Under 'Remarks', it is noted that he was discharged in May 1915. Entries in this column may record whether the soldier was a prisoner of war (P of W) or killed in action (K in A). Use the Medal Roll key in WO 329/1 to convert the "Roll" reference into a WO 329 volume number which you order up on the computer ordering system as an original document.

WO 329/1 British War and Victory Medals - entry for 14th London Regiment

BW & V Medals			
Unit	Folios	OW Index No. 5	Vol Nos.
14th LONDON REGT	1-315	TP 14/101B-3	B.928
	316-630	TP 14/3-4	B.929

WO 329 Class List

WO 329		
1928	14th London Regiment (London Scottish)	B.928

The medal roll entry in WO 329/1928 for Ronald Colman is reproduced as fig 12.

Chapter 8. Private William Henry Richards - a case study with no service records

8.1 Introduction

We had long known about my wife's great-grandfather William Henry Richards (see fig. 13). He was Welsh, a painter and decorator by trade and he died in the First World War. We had seen three of his letters home, one of them to his little daughter, Beatie. Henry's letters show that he often sent small presents home to his daughter and her friend (see fig. 15). His wife and sister-in-law were sent embroidered handkerchiefs and Henry was anxious to learn whether they had arrived safely. In return, Lily would send cakes or pudding and Henry and his mates would consider these a real treat as the food at the front, although good, was not plentiful. There was little more to the story than this, but we hoped to find out a lot more. The key problem was to identify which military unit he served with and, as his service record has not survived, it was not possible to easily confirm this from other conflicting evidence. Records show that he served with both the 14th and 17th Battalions of the Welch Regiment. Without being certain of his date of transfer from one battalion to the other, all the entries in the War Diaries of these units seem a little hollow. They tell of the events experienced by the men of both battalions while they were serving on different parts of the front but we cannot be sure with which one Henry found himself at any particular time. One of his letters is headed 'Attached 14th Welsh. 6 IBD BEF France'. Research has shown, however, that he must have been with the 17th Battalion when he died. In accordance with the policy of the time, he is buried near to where he fell - definitely within a quarter of a mile, possibly even nearer.

8.2 The key sources

The first official document we obtained was the death certificate from St Catherine's House (see 5.5 and **fig 14**). This mentioned the 14th Battalion, Welch Regiment which accorded with all three surviving letters from him which said either '14th Welsh' or 'att(ached to) 14th Welsh'.

Another early enquiry was to the Commonwealth War Graves Commission (CWGC). They hold details of every person killed on service during the two World Wars. This information chiefly concerns the place of burial or the memorial if there is no known grave. Very often, though, they can give personal details. On this occasion, the CWGC was able to provide name, rank and number, cemetery name and location, grave number and details of next of kin. The CWGC quoted the same details of Henry's unit as were printed on the Certificate 'In Everlasting Memory' which was issued after the War, i.e. his battalion is given as the 17th. This was surely correct at the time of Henry's death. The sources agree on his date of death as 24 April 1917 and on this date the 14th Battalion were not in action. Their War Diary (WO 95/2559) shows that they were in training and suffered

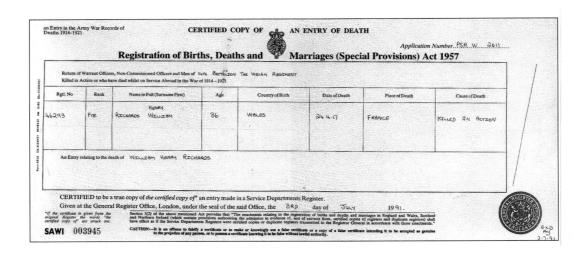

Fig 13(above) Private W H Richards (private collection-Stuart Tamblin)

Fig 14(below) Death certificate of W H Richards (Office of National Statistics. The design of this certificate is Crown copyright and is reproduced with the permission of the Controller of SO)

no casualties for several days on either side of 24 April.

Strangely, *Soldiers Died*, (see 2.3) shows Henry with the 14th Battalion but the War Diaries for the 17th (WO 95/2607) do tend to confirm that he died fighting with the latter. They not only record the loss of a number of 'other ranks' but the action described was near Fifteen Ravine (see map - fig 13), in whose cemetery Henry rests. It seems most likely that Henry went out with the 14th Battalion but later joined the 17th, possibly not long before his death. This would tally with an entry in the War Diary of the 17th for 2 April 1917 which records a transfer into the battalion of eighty-five men. Unfortunately, the 14th's Diary does not contain a corresponding entry to confirm a transfer out.

The mystery might have been solved with the aid of his service record. The Ministry of Defence at Hayes searched for it in the 'Burnt Documents' series (see 1.1) but it must have been one of the many which were lost in the bombing during the Second World War. A set of pension records, the 'Unburnt Documents' (see 1.2) is also kept at Hayes to be cross checked automatically when the service record has been lost but nothing at all was found.

The Medal Rolls at the Public Record Office (WO 329) only record Henry's service with the 17th Battalion, whose War Diary, together with those for the Brigade and Division to which it belonged, is therefore the main source of information about his war service.

Sources at the Public Record Office

Medal Rolls	WO 329/1324	Welch Regiment
Orders of Battle	WO 95/5468	France, 1916-1917
War Diaries	WO 95/2559	14th Battalion, Welch Regiment
	WO 95/2592-2616	40th Division
	WO 95/2604	119th Brigade HQ
	WO 95/2607	17th Battalion, Welch Regiment
Trench Maps	WO 297/3748	Villers-Plouich 1917
	WO 153/1209	Villers-Plouich and Hindenburg Line 1918
Readers' Guides	No. 2	*Army Records for Family Historians* by Simon Fowler
Information Leaflets	No. 6	*Army Operations, 1914-1919*
	No. 59	*Army Genealogy*
	No. 101	*Service Medal Rolls, 1914-1918*
	No. 115	*Military Maps of the First World War*

Soldiers Died In The Great War - Part 45 - The Welch Regiment. (Microfilm)

Personal Sources

Letters home from Private 46293 W H Richards.

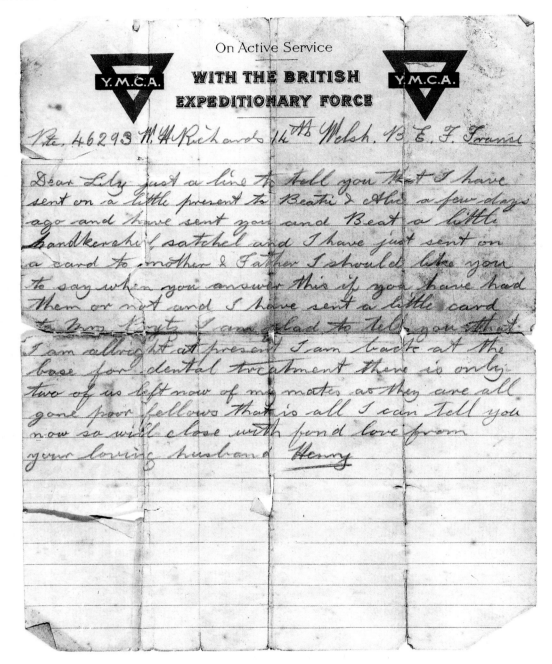

Fig 15 Letter from W H Richards (private collection-Stuart Tamblin)

Office of National Statistics

Birth, marriage and death certificates.

8.3 War Diaries and Trench Maps

War Diary of the 14th Battalion, Welch Regiment - WO 95/2559

The 14th Battalion of the Welch Regiment was originally raised at Swansea by the Mayor and Corporation of Swansea with the Swansea Football and Cricket Club. On 2 December 1915, the War Diary records that it left Winchester Camp, where it had been in training, for Southampton, to embark for Le Havre. Seventeen hours later, it disembarked and marched to the transit camp at Bléville, before continuing to the station. At 4pm on 5 December, the battalion arrived at its billets in Crecques and joined the 114th Infantry Brigade. Over Christmas 1915, the four companies of the 14th Welch were attached to the different battalions of the 57th Brigade for 'instruction in the trenches' and suffered their first casualties - one dead and seven wounded.

In the first three months of 1916, the battalion moved between Robecq, Neuve Chapelle, Richbourg and Givenchy sometimes in the front line, sometimes in reserve. At the end of March, the men were inspected by Brigadier General Marden. The day also featured a demonstration of the capabilities of the German flame thrower or 'Flammenwerfer'. On 30 March General Monro, commanding officer of the First Army, followed up with an inspection of the whole brigade.

On 10 July, during the battle of the Somme, the 17th Battalion, as part of the 114th Brigade, was ordered to capture Mametz Wood. It suffered 376 casualties in the attack and was awarded two Military Crosses and two Military Medals, one of which was to Sergeant Buse (see 7.5).

From September 1916 to March 1917, the battalion served in the Ypres salient but took part in no major offensive. The War Diary records service in the front line and reserve trenches, a trench raid on November 17th, when 20 prisoners were taken, and Christmas Day spent in Corps Reserve Camp. Christmas dinner was served at 1 o'clock, followed by a concert at 4.30 in the YMCA hut.

At one stage, Henry took an enforced break from military duties to go to the base camp for dental treatment. It is not recorded which was the lesser of the two evils. At this time, he woefully records in a letter home that out of all his mates, there only remained himself and one other (fig. 15).

War Diary of the 17th Battalion, Welch Regiment - WO 95/2607

On 2 June 1916, the 995 men and 35 officers of the 17th Battalion left Blackdown Barracks for Southampton to embark for Le Havre. On the fifth, they entrained for Lillers and marched from there to billets in St Hilaire. They joined the 119th Infantry Brigade and 40th Division.

The 17th Battalion, under Lieutenant Colonel C J Wilkie, spent June and July 1916 at Barlin, Bully Grenay and Calonne and matched the 14th's achievements with a Military Medal for the gallantry shown by Lance Corporal E Stiff. August saw a move to Loos and the men were mostly in or near the front line throughout the month. The War Diary recorded that 'the whole system of trenches is in very bad order, very little shelter for men in the front line, in places none at all, and dugouts in support line quite insufficient. There is practically no wire on our front but the enemy wire is thick and in very good order with no obvious gaps in it'.

The battalion remained in the line in September and much of October, in frequent danger from aerial darts, rifle grenades and gas shells. Sentries were posted and became very skilful at minimising casualties by spotting attacks and giving warnings. On 18 October, both the Commanding Officer and his second in command were killed by a high explosive shell. November was spent out of the front line, resting in billets at Ternas and Boisbergues and training. In 'Camp 12' at Bois Celestins, the battalion let Christmas Day pass very quietly. Extra rations of cigarettes and other small luxuries were issued. They returned to the forward trenches south of Rancourt on 27 December. By the end of this tour of duty, 113 men had been hospitalised with 'trench foot'.

Much of February was spent training and in reserve. At Camp III - 'Belair', the men celebrated St David's Day with dinner at 5 pm and a concert at 7 pm, 'thoroughly enjoyed by all ranks'. The officers continued their celebrations into a second day when they held a regimental dinner at 8 pm on 2 March. The rest of March was spent in and out of the line at Clery and Haut-Allaenes. On 2 April 1917, the 17th Battalion received a draft of 85 men. It is believed that this must be when Henry transferred from the 14th Battalion.

To supplement the account given in the war diary of the battalion, and to appreciate the wider strategic objectives, one can use the war diaries of the Brigade (119th Brigade HQ - WO 95/2604) and of the Division (40th Division - WO 95/2592-2616) to which it belonged. On 17 April, the Brigade moved up to the Divisional front with the 17th Welch held in reserve at Fins and then in support at Queen's Cross. On 20 April, the 40th Division was ordered to attack and occupy a line one and three-quarter miles wide running to the south-west of Villers-Plouich and Beaucamp and incorporating Fifteen Ravine. It ran broadly parallel to the Hindenburg line, little more than a mile away. The 119th Brigade was to take a spur running for four hundred yards on the right flank and the Ravine itself - fully half of the overall objective. The main attack was planned for April 24th and orders (WO

95/2604) were issued from Brigade Headquarters to all commanding officers.

```
             119th INFANTRY BRIGADE ORDER NO. 87

Ref. Map. No. T.S. 52, 1/20, 000      (already forwarded
to those
directly concerned).

1.   The 40th Division will assault the Villages of VILLERS
     PLOUICH and BEAUCAMP and gain a footing in R.14.central,
     R.7.central on April 24th.

2.   The 119th Infantry Brigade will attack on the Right
     and the 120th Infantry Brigade on the Left, Boundary
     between Brigades - a line from R.19.a.0.7 to R.14.b.1.8.

3.     OBJECTIVES

  (a)    119th Infantry Brigade :-

         The spur R.21.c.5.0. - R.21.a.1.1. - R.14.c.8.0 -
         trenches on Spur R.14.b.3.0 - R.14.b.2.8.
         (exclusive)

  (b)    120th Infantry Brigade :-

         Ravine R.14.b.2.8. (inclusive) - R.8.c.8.6 -
         R.7.central - Q.12.central - Q.11.b.9.0 - thence
         to their present left.
```

The objective now was to advance another half-mile or mile beyond the Ravine and push the enemy back beyond Villers-Plouich and Beaucamp. With the 120th Brigade on the left, the 119th Brigade was to operate on the right, to the south-east of the villages. Within the brigade, the 18th Welch were to push on the right flank, the 17th on the left. The specific instructions to the 17th Battalion in this order were that -

```
The 17th Welsh Regt, will attack on the Left Brigade front
with two companies in line of column of platoons, and two
Companies in Support. It will march by its left.
  O.C. 17th Welsh Regt, will arrange to thin his line if
the objectives are gained with small loss.
  He will further arrange for mopping up parties to deal
with all places where the enemy is entrenched.
  He will have the call upon the 19th R.W.Fusiliers in case
of necessity.
```

In the attack, the infantry in fighting order, were each to carry two grenades, two flares, two sandbags, a filled water bottle and iron rations. The flares were to be lit when requested by contact aeroplanes. Once they had reached their objective, the troops had to create strong-points and then clear the trench known as 'Cornwall Cut' (see map, fig. 17, square R.14). This done, the 17th would be very near to the top of the hill which faced them.

The extract from a trench map illustrated as fig. 17 (WO 153/1209) shows the Hindenburg line (square R.10), Villiers Plouich (square R.13), Fifteen Ravine (square R.19) and Queen's Cross (square Q.28). The map is divided into large squares, each designated by a letter of the alphabet, and then sub-divided into 36 smaller squares, numbered in sequence. Each of these smaller squares is further sub-divided into 4 squares, a, b, c and d, as illustrated on the map in square Q.6, and each of these smallest of squares has a notched scale of 1-10 running along the side, so that an absolutely precise reference can be given. Thus, on the map illustrated, the centre point of the letter Q would bear the full reference Q.6.b.5.5. References like this appear frequently in the War Diaries.

On 23 April, the 17th Battalion moved into position at Fifteen Ravine, poised for the main attack at 4.15 am on the following morning. At Zero Hour, they moved forward under the effective protective barrage of the 181st Brigade, Royal Field Artillery. There was a counter barrage from the enemy but this one was 'comparatively ineffective', partly due to the troops having already advanced out of the forward trenches. After six minutes, the British barrage started to creep forward at the rate of a hundred yards every four minutes. Within twenty minutes, the 17th Welch, and the 120th Brigade on their left, passed the initial objective and two companies started to dig in. They were positioned in front of a road east-north-east of Villers-Plouich which was only a hundred yards short of the final objective. The advance was temporarily held up by uncut wire and on the right, the battalion came under hostile fire from both rifles and machine guns. This they returned and eventually found a gap through the wire. They reached their objective and began to bomb 'Cornwall Cut'. An hour later, at 7.05 am, all objectives had been reached, right across the Brigade front. The village of Villers-Plouich had been taken by 120th Brigade but was then heavily shelled by the Germans at 9.40. It was consequently evacuated but the British were able to consolidate and form strong points elsewhere. Shortly after noon, the trenches were cleared of Germans and things fell quiet. Sixty-one prisoners and a machine gun had been taken by the Brigade, including one officer and thirty-nine men by the 17th Welch.

It is recorded that 'all ranks behaved with the utmost gallantry and dash ... the advance under the barrage was made cooly (*sic*) and steadily as on a parade ground'. William Henry Richards was almost certainly among twenty-seven ORs and one officer killed in the battalion. A further sixty-one were wounded. Brigadier General Crozier issued a 'Special Order of the Day' on 25 April: 'GOC 119th Infantry Brigade wishes to thank all ranks of the Brigade which he has the honour to command on the success of their operations on the 21st and 24th April 1917 and to congratulate them on the valour displayed. The gaining of all the objectives and the retention of same throughout was only made possible by the united co-operation of all ...' The forward line now held was on high ground overlooking the Hindenburg Line. Half a mile away, from a slightly less elevated position at La Vacquerie, a machine gun had troubled the British. Two days after Henry's death, it was finally put out of action and the Welsh were free to name the summit 'Rhondda Hill'. The Germans had lost a lot of ground and were known to be only 600 yards away. Patrols were frequently sent out but the battalion survived six consecutive days in the new forward positions without seeing the enemy at all. It was relieved at the end of the month and moved back into Brigade Reserve for some much needed time in billets in Equancourt.

Henry was laid to rest at the edge of a field which became Fifteen Ravine British Cemetery. It is to the east of Villers-Plouich and on the south side of the road to La Vacquerie. His grave is number 27 in Row C, Plot 1.

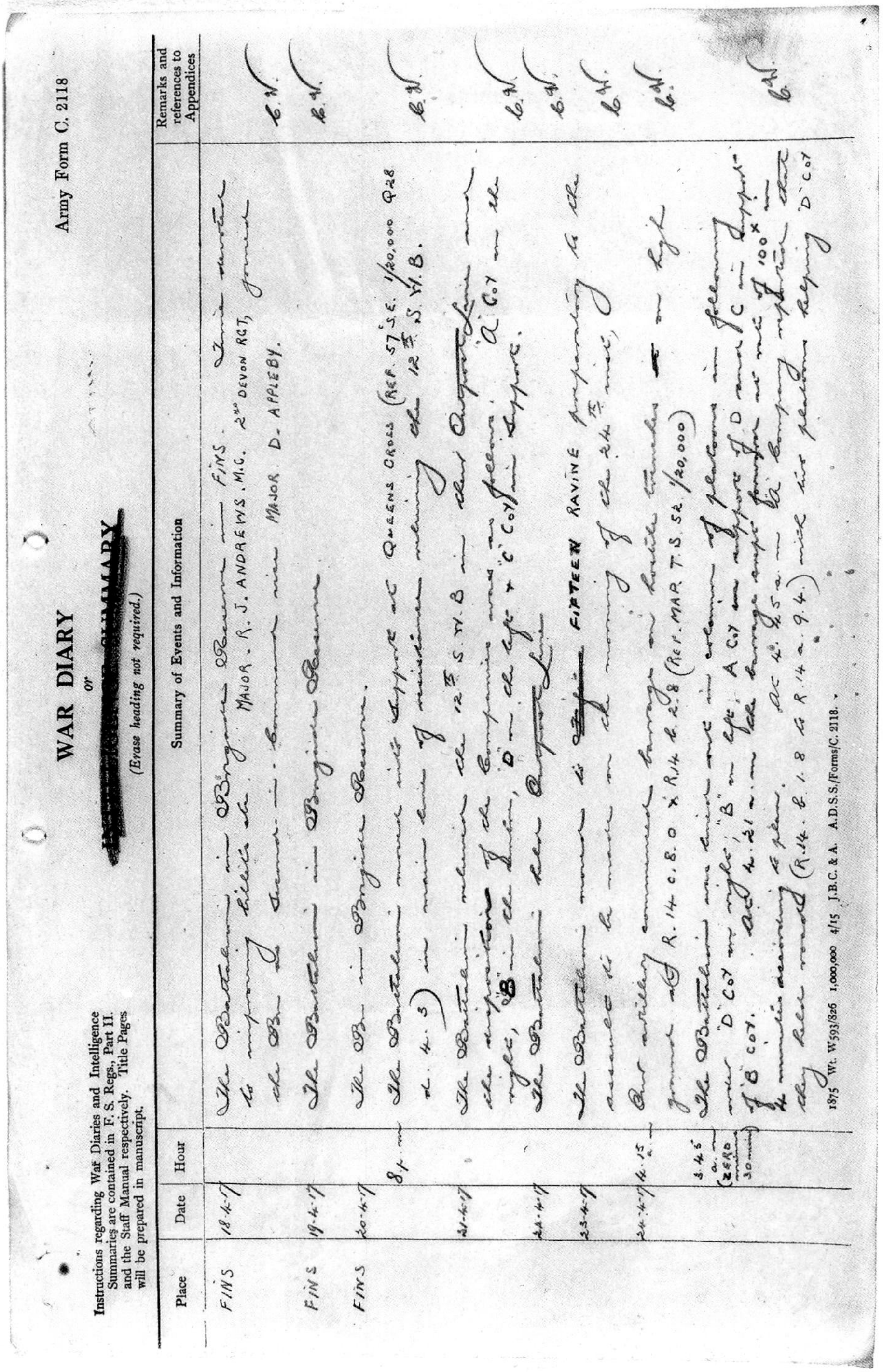

WAR DIARY

or

INTELLIGENCE SUMMARY

(Erase heading not required.)

Army Form C. 2118

Instructions regarding War Diaries and Intelligence Summaries are contained in F. S. Regs., Part II. and the Staff Manual respectively. Title Pages will be prepared in manuscript.

Place	Date	Hour	Summary of Events and Information	Remarks and references to Appendices

1875 Wt. W593/826 1,000,000 4/15 J.B.C. & A. A.D.S.S./Forms/C. 2118.

Fig 16 17th Battalion, Welch Regiment, War Diary entry (WO 95/ 2607)

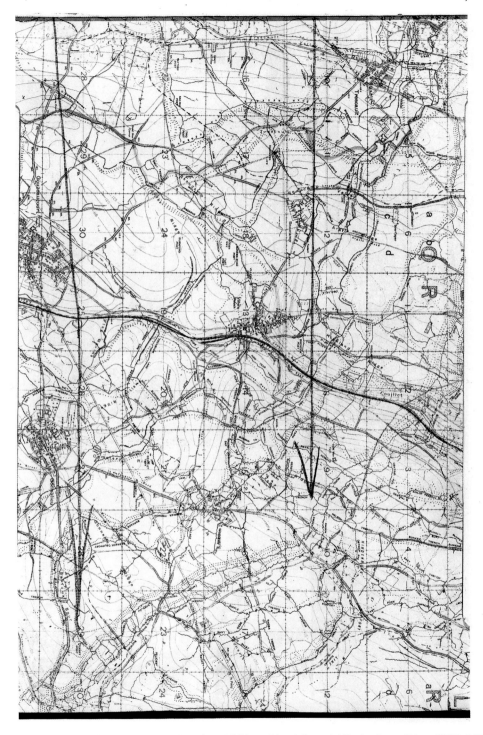

Fig 17 Section of Trench Map showing Villiers-Plouich and Hindenburg Line (WO 153/ 1209)

Chapter 9: Gunner Philip Pearn - a case study with Service Records

9.1 Introduction

In tracing the military career of someone who survived the First World War, after taking heed of information spread by word of mouth in the family, it is often the man's medals which are of use in providing details. At the Public Record Office, an index is held to the man's entitlement in the form of a microfiche copy of a card index (see 7.7). This in turn leads to the original medal rolls. In the case of my grandmother's brother, Philip Pearn, I learned from these that he served with the Royal Garrison Artillery with the service number 133020 and the rank of Gunner (WO 329/284). Any further information would come principally from his personal service record, if it had survived.

9.2 The Service Records in WO 363 'Burnt Documents' series

The Service Record for Philip Pearn, who fought with the Royal Garrison Artillery (RGA) forms part of the collection of 'Burnt Documents'

Fig 18 Gunner Philip Pearn (standing) at Thorpe Hospital, Norwich (private collection-Stuart Tamblin)

(described in 1.1). It comprises a small file of documents which starts with "List of Transfer Documents", covers his 'Short Service' attestation and statement of services and ends with an 'Inside Sheet' which details the occasions when he was added to the casualty lists and went to hospital back in 'Blighty'. The original papers are both singed and water-damaged (see fig. 19) and are not yet open to public inspection. Note that his original service number, 1927, was later changed to 133020. This new number can faintly be seen in pencil above the number 1927 on the form illustrated.

The papers give many details of use to the genealogist and military historian alike. There is information about his home address and pre-war occupation, his parents and his wife whom he married while on leave just after the armistice. The record covers a number of aspects of service life, from attestation and taking the oath of allegiance, through many months of active service, shelling the enemy and being shelled and gassed, to the issue of his medals and a Protection Certificate issued after demobilisation.

1) List of Transfer Documents

This is a comprehensive tick-sheet, with just a few items marked, such as conduct sheet, clothing return, medical history sheet and active service casualty form. Not all of these have remained in the file. It records that Philip was transferred to 275 Siege Battery on 1 November 1916.

2) Enlistment & Statement of Services Record Army Form B.2512

This is a large sheet of paper, folded vertically to form a four-page booklet.

a) Short Service Attestation

"For the Duration of the War, with the Colours and in the Army Reserve", Philip enlisted into the Devonshire RGA (Royal Garrison Artillery) and was given the official number 1927. Upon attestation, he was asked a number of questions and his basic details were recorded. He was a British subject, aged twenty years and two months from Widegates, Hessenford, St Germans, Cornwall. He was unmarried and a horseman. Never having served before in HM Forces, he had now "received a notice" from a Captain W A Jenkin and stated that he was willing to serve for the duration of the War.

The document was signed by H G Hawken, a Justice of the Peace in Liskeard and forwarded to the headquarters of the Devonshire RGA where it was processed on 5 June 1916 when Philip was called up from the Reserve. This date was later recorded in another document as Philip's date of enlistment.

b) Descriptive Report on Enlistment

Here, a number of details are repeated and we additionally learn of Philip's height (5'9½') and chest measurement (37½' + 4' expansion), his father's name, Harry and then the details of his marriage, although these were added later. He was married to Amelia Nicholas, a spinster of Layland, Morval at the parish church on 25 November 1918.

The Military History Sheet carries on from here and includes precise details of his dates of service and tells that he was wounded and entered on War Office Casualty List HA 11263 and eventually awarded the British War and Victory Medals (for which a receipt dated 9 October 1921 is attached).

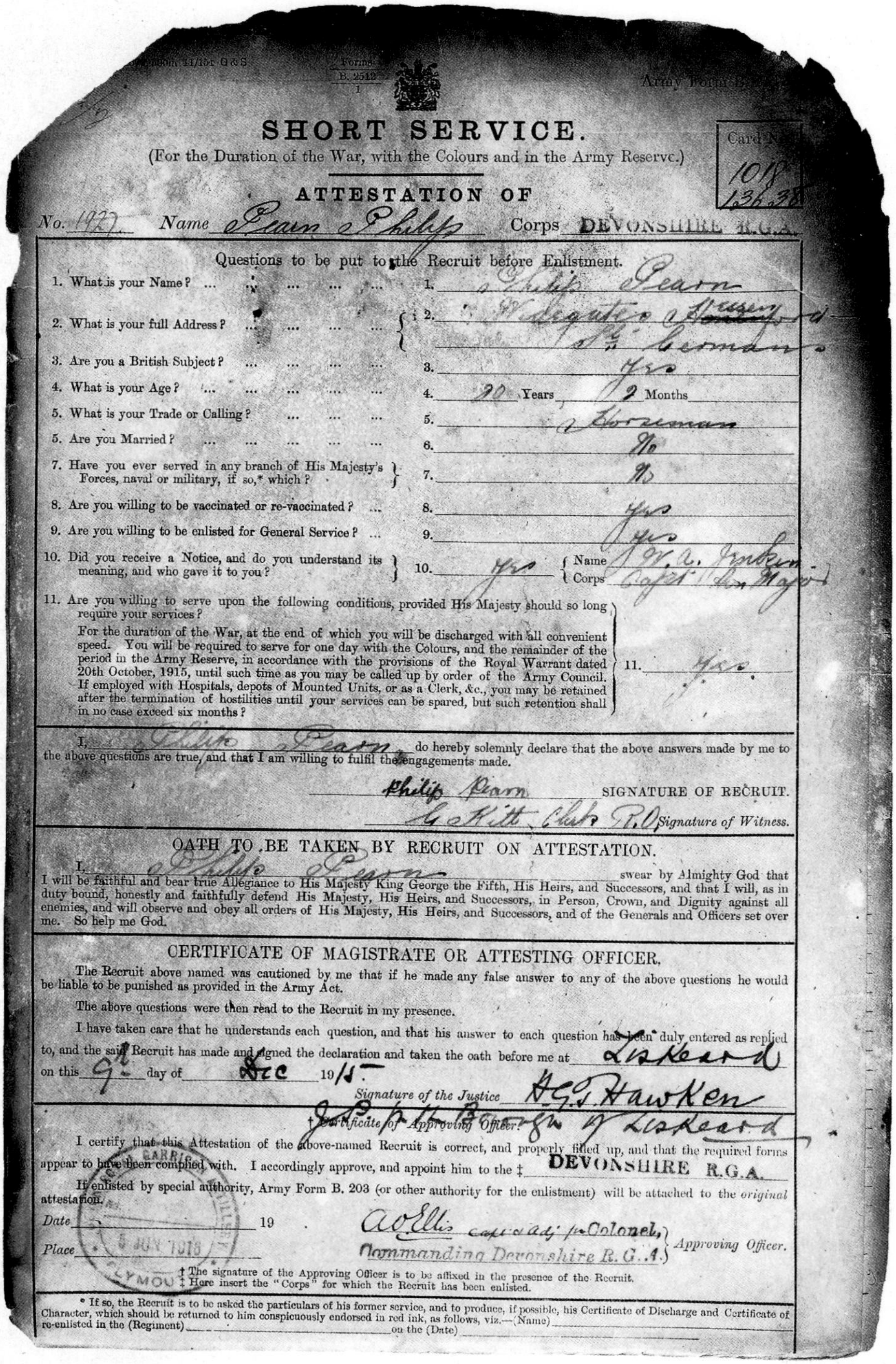

Forms B. 2512 / 1

Army Form B. 2512

Card No. 1018 / 136138

SHORT SERVICE.

(For the Duration of the War, with the Colours and in the Army Reserve.)

ATTESTATION OF

No. 1927 Name Pearn Philip Corps DEVONSHIRE R.G.A.

Questions to be put to the Recruit before Enlistment.

1. What is your Name? ... 1. Philip Pearn
2. What is your full Address? ... 2. Westgate, St Germans
3. Are you a British Subject? ... 3. Yes
4. What is your Age? ... 4. 20 Years 2 Months
5. What is your Trade or Calling? ... 5. Horseman
5. Are you Married? ... 6. No
7. Have you ever served in any branch of His Majesty's Forces, naval or military, if so,* which? 7. No
8. Are you willing to be vaccinated or re-vaccinated? ... 8. Yes
9. Are you willing to be enlisted for General Service? ... 9. Yes
10. Did you receive a Notice, and do you understand its meaning, and who gave it to you? 10. Yes Name ... Corps ...
11. Are you willing to serve upon the following conditions, provided His Majesty should so long require your services? For the duration of the War, at the end of which you will be discharged with all convenient speed. You will be required to serve for one day with the Colours, and the remainder of the period in the Army Reserve, in accordance with the provisions of the Royal Warrant dated 20th October, 1915, until such time as you may be called up by order of the Army Council. If employed with Hospitals, depots of Mounted Units, or as a Clerk, &c., you may be retained after the termination of hostilities until your services can be spared, but such retention shall in no case exceed six months? 11. Yes

I, Philip Pearn do hereby solemnly declare that the above answers made by me to the above questions are true, and that I am willing to fulfil the engagements made.

Philip Pearn SIGNATURE OF RECRUIT.

G. Kitt, Clerk R.O. *Signature of Witness.*

OATH TO BE TAKEN BY RECRUIT ON ATTESTATION.

I, Philip Pearn swear by Almighty God that I will be faithful and bear true Allegiance to His Majesty King George the Fifth, His Heirs, and Successors, and that I will, as in duty bound, honestly and faithfully defend His Majesty, His Heirs, and Successors, in Person, Crown, and Dignity against all enemies, and will observe and obey all orders of His Majesty, His Heirs, and Successors, and of the Generals and Officers set over me. So help me God.

CERTIFICATE OF MAGISTRATE OR ATTESTING OFFICER.

The Recruit above named was cautioned by me that if he made any false answer to any of the above questions he would be liable to be punished as provided in the Army Act.

The above questions were then read to the Recruit in my presence.

I have taken care that he understands each question, and that his answer to each question has been duly entered as replied to, and the said Recruit has made and signed the declaration and taken the oath before me at Liskeard on this 9th day of Dec 1915.

Signature of the Justice H.G.T. Hawken J.P. Borough of Liskeard

† *Certificate of Approving Officer.*

I certify that this Attestation of the above-named Recruit is correct, and properly filled up, and that the required forms appear to have been complied with. I accordingly approve, and appoint him to the ‡ DEVONSHIRE R.G.A.

If enlisted by special authority, Army Form B. 203 (or other authority for the enlistment) will be attached to the *original* attestation.

Date ... 19 ... A.O. Ellis ... Colonel, Commanding Devonshire R.G.A. } *Approving Officer.*

Place ...

5 JUN 1916 PLYMOUTH

† The signature of the Approving Officer is to be affixed in the presence of the Recruit.
‡ Here insert the "Corps" for which the Recruit has been enlisted.

* If so, the Recruit is to be asked the particulars of his former service, and to produce, if possible, his Certificate of Discharge and Certificate of Character, which should be returned to him conspicuously endorsed in red ink, as follows, viz.—(Name) ... re-enlisted in the (Regiment) ... on the (Date) ...

Fig 19 Gunner Philip Pearn - Army Form B.2512 (WO 363, piece number not yet assigned)

The dates are given under the heading "Campaigns including Actions." He served at home from 5 June 1916; with the BEF (British Expeditionary Force in France) from 15 March 1917; the "Home Brigade" again from 7 July 1917 (when he was wounded); the BEF again from 19 November 1917 and finally at home from 26 January 1919 until demobilisation on 23 February.

c) Statement of Services

Confirming the above details, this document shows that Philip attested on 9 December 1915 and was placed in the Army Reserve on 10 December. There is no date for mobilisation as such but he was posted with the rank of Gunner on 5 June 1916 to 275 Siege Battery, RGA. When wounded, he was attached to the Clearing Office (7 July 1917) and then to 2 Reinforcement Siege Depot on 16 October. Back with the BEF the next month, he was transferred to 30 Siege Battery on 25 November. He was transferred to Class 'Z' Reserve on 23 February 1919, rated fit A1. The dates have been repeated in pencil on the reverse, with the additional note that Philip came home from 20 November 1918 for fourteen days' leave. This was the time when he was married.

3) Protection Certificate and Certificate of Identity Army Form Z.11

Again repeating Philip's basic details such as date of birth and address, this document shows that he passed through No 1 Dispersal Unit, Purfleet on 26 January 1919. He had served in theatre of war code number 1a (i.e. France and Belgium, see 7.8), been graded fit A1 and told to rejoin at Plymouth in case of future emergency.

4) "Inside Sheet" Army Form B.104-53

This loose-leaf addition to the attestation document gives some very specific information relating to Philip's wound and admission to hospitals in France and England. War Office Casualty list numbers are quoted but unfortunately, these have not survived in the records at the PRO. Returning to the BEF for the last year of the war, Philip's release on agricultural grounds was finally requested by H Pearce of Widegates.

9.3 War Diaries and Hospital Records

Collating all the information contained in the documents in WO 363, we can record the following chronology.

9 December 1915	Attested at Liskeard and placed in the Reserve
5 June 1916	Posted to the Devonshire RGA (Home Brigade) as Gunner {for basic training}
1 November 1916	Attached to 275 Siege Battery, RGA {for specific training and preparation for the Western Front}

15 March 1917	British Expeditionary Force, France {front-line action}
2 July 1917	No 3 Canadian General Hospital, Boulogne {shell wound in left hip}
7 July 1917	Thorpe Hospital, Norwich, Norfolk
16 October 1917	No 2 Reinforcement Siege Depot, Catterick {awaiting posting to the front line again}
20 November 1917	British Expeditionary Force, France
25 November 1917	30 Siege Battery, RGA
20 November 1918	Home Brigade {fourteen days' leave, during which he married}
4 December 1918	Rejoin BEF
26 January 1919	Home - No 1 Dispersal Unit, Purfleet
23 February 1919	Class Z Reserve.

Although this list gives a lot of information on Philip's time in the Army, we have so far discovered little about the front-line action which he saw. For this, we need to turn to the War Diaries in WO 95 and concentrate on 275 Siege Battery after 15 March 1917, number 3 Canadian General Hospital and 30 Siege Battery after November 1917.

Unfortunately, it seems that no records for Thorpe Hospital, Norwich survive. Neither is there any relevant entry in the PRO Medical Records Project card index which is available in the Research Enquiries Room. Many medical records such as admissions and operations registers and medical history sheets were analysed by the authorities and have survived in Class MH 106. However, their coverage is selective and it appears that nothing still exists for either the RGA or the two hospitals. Although the registers for No 3 Canadian General Hospital are not available, the War Diary is and this gives information as to location and summaries as to cases. A photograph of Philip from this time is reproduced at fig. 18.

From the WO 95 class list, it appears that the war diaries of both 30 and 275 Siege Battery are missing, except for a few months. For 275 Siege Battery, the unit's diaries are only available in the PRO for December 1917 (WO 95/225), after Philip had left them. Number 30 Siege Battery fares little better with only those for August to November 1915 (WO 95/322) surviving, well before Philip's service. These diaries may, however, contain useful information about other units with which they served, as may the Orders of Battle (WO 95/5467 to 5469 for France) and the last piece in the class - WO 95/5494 - which lists locations and dates for many of the miscellaneous and non-infantry units.

275 Siege Battery, RGA

WO 95/225 only contains the 275 Siege Battery War Diary for one month but WO 95/5494 lists all batteries numerically and gives a paragraph or two of information about each. It shows that 275 Siege Battery went out to the Western Front in March 1917. Arriving in France, it became part of the 51st HAG (Heavy Artillery Group or Brigade) on 29 March 1917, transferring to 53rd HAG on 17 May. Philip left 275 Battery in July (when wounded), but the unit went on to serve with the 66th HAG and then 50th HAG (50th South African Brigade.) The Battery originally comprised four 8' howitzers but was made up to six guns in June 1917.

3 Canadian General Hospital, Boulogne

The WO 95 class list shows the Hospital under 'Lines of Communication' rather than with the front-line units. War Diaries are available for March 1915 to April 1919 in WO 95/4093.

July started with clear and bright weather and on 2 July, when Philip arrived, Dominion Day (1 July) was still being celebrated. Sir Arthur T Sloggett, Director General of Medical Services, British Armies in France, was present at the sports day and showed a keen interest in the hospital orchestra.

On 3 July, Sir Arthur was joined by Surgeon General R H S Sawyer when the Hospital was honoured by a visit from Her Majesty Queen Mary. She inspected several wards, conversing with many patients and was very much pleased with all that she saw. She wished the Hospital continued success.

The War Diary records little else relevant to Philip Pearn at this time but does seem to list occurrences of notifiable diseases and gives post-mortem reports on important cases. Wounds, as opposed to illnesses, were too numerous to mention but are summarised monthly. In July 1917, the Hospital received 3418 cases and admitted 2820. There were sixteen deaths and 200 operations.

30 Siege Battery, RGA

Philip returned to the BEF in November 1917 and was transferred to 30 Siege Battery. The unit remained at rest and in training until Boxing Day and then joined 59th HAG for the rest of the War. The Orders of Battle, WO 95/5469 (1 February 1918), show that 30 Siege Battery also had six 8' howitzers and was attached to 59th Brigade (RGA). Although the War Diary of 30 Siege Battery has not survived, it is possible to use the Orders of Battle to establish its main sphere of operations for the rest of 1918.

In November 1918, Philip came home on fourteen days' leave to be married but was back with his unit by 4 December. He was demobilised on 23 February 1919, eventually settled in Widegates near Looe in Cornwall, and died in 1979.

Chapter 10. Lieutenant Siegfried Sassoon : A case study

As with other ranks, it was possible for more than one individual with exactly the same name to have held a commission during the First World War. Although it is much easier to identify an individual officer, there are additional sources available which record information about him.

The Army List

The *Army List* has been in existence since the 18th century and editions have been produced over a number of different periods; Half Yearly, Quarterly and Monthly. Although the Half Yearly and Quarterly editions have their own individual merits, for the First World War period the most useful are probably those *Army Lists* which were produced monthly.

The purpose of the monthly *Army List* was to show the distribution of officers on the active list of the Regular Army, the Royal Marines, Special Reserve, Territorial Force and Reserve of Officers, in which unit where they were serving and their seniority (i.e. the date of their last promotion). Each *Army List* has a name index which provides the page or column number on which details of an individual will be found.

Unless the date on which an individual was first commissioned is known, then it may be necessary to look at a number of *Army Lists* until an entry for the individual is found.

Siegfried Sassoon first appears in the Monthly *Army List* for June 1915, with the following entry.

Index R   Sassoon S. L.   1116 b

It is possible to find a number of prefixes alongside the name of the individual you seek. These prefixes denote into which part of the army the individual was commissioned. The most common are:

> M Militia
> R Special Reserve of Officers
> T Territorial Force
> V Volunteers
> Y Yeomanry

If there is no prefix, the individual was commissioned into the regular army.

Turning to column 1116 b of the June 1915 *Army List*, the entry for Siegfried Sassoon provides the following information:

3rd Battalion (Reserve) Royal Welch Fusiliers
Sassoon S. L. 29 May 15
(on probation)

From this entry, we can see into which regiment Siegfried Sassoon was commissioned and the date of that commission. Note the entry for Robert Graves in the same column.

By following the career of an officer in the *Army List* it is possible to note when he was promoted and to which units he was posted.

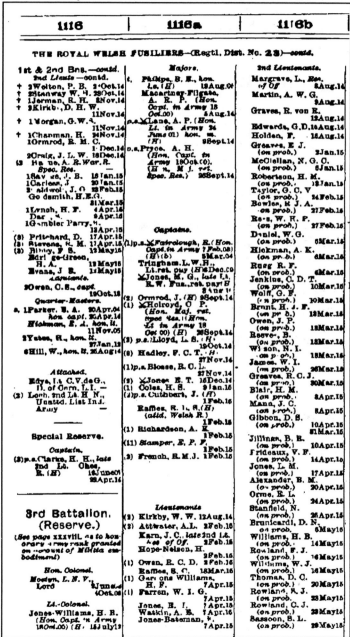

Fig 20 Army List entry for Siegfried Sassoon

Commissions and Appointments: Using the *London Gazette*.

The date which follows the name of an individual in the *Army List,* is the date on which the particular commission was granted. To find the announcement of all promotions, appointments and the resignation or relinquishment of a commission, it is necessary to look at the *London Gazette* (ZJ 1). In each quarterly index of the *London Gazette*, under the heading of State Intelligence, is a section called Military Promotions and Appointments. Within this section are further subsections which are the same as the prefixes which can be found in the *Army List* (see above). Once the name of an individual is found, the page number alongside that individual has to be converted into the relevant *London Gazette* entry.

The announcement of the commission of Siegfried Sassoon as a Second Lieutenant in the Special Reserve of Officers (Infantry) for service with 3 Battalion Royal Welch Fusiliers, can be found on page 5115 of the *London Gazette* for June 1915 (ZJ 1/622).

If an officer resigned his commission on medical grounds or was dismissed as the result of a court martial, details were published in the *London Gazette*.

War Diaries

The purpose of the war diary was to record the day to day activities of a unit. In most cases, the names of officers are far more likely to appear than those of other ranks. However, it was really up to the regimental adjutant or nominated officer as to what was entered into the diary apart from what was really necessary.

Second Lieutenant Siegfried Sassoon first appears in the war diary of the 1st Battalion Royal Welch Fusiliers on 24 November 1915, when he is recorded as having arrived for service on the Western Front (WO 95/1665). Sassoon is next noted on 11 April 1916 as having met with and dispersed an enemy patrol.

By working through war diaries, it may be possible to create a partial picture of what an individual officer did during his time both in and out of the trenches.

Medal Records

11/07/19

Name	Corps	Reg. No.	Rank	Date of Discharge	Cause of Discharge
Sassoon M.C. Siefried Lorraine	R Welsh Fus 3rd		Capt	Enlistment	BW+VM: VOL: C311 PAGE: 591C 1914-15 STAR VOL: C940 PAGE: 37/A

Date of application (a) Badge (b) Medal 28-9-61

No. of File " 122091/6

Address of applicant :– Weirleigh Matfield, Kent

BW+VM

Action taken ISSUED: IV 3030 DATE 15-7-85

Eligible 20 2 19. 1914-15 STAR ISSUED IV. 3039 DATE 22/7/85

W0749—46/26 200,000 8/17 HWV(P88) K638
1528—JCP2055 700,000(25) 6/18

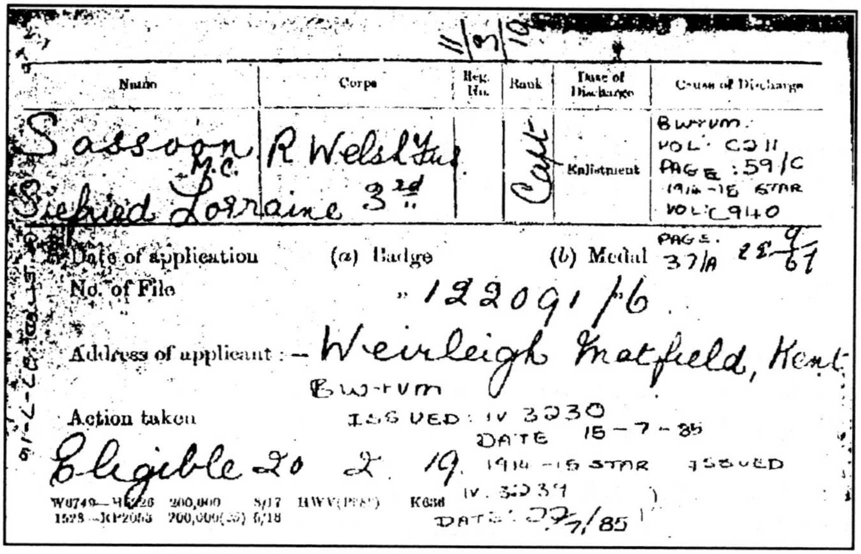

Fig 21 Silver War Badge, Index card (WO 372)

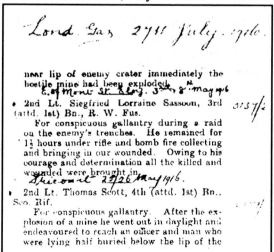

Unlike other ranks, whose medals were sent automatically, officers had to apply for their campaign medals. This is the main reason why it is sometimes impossible for a medal index card to be located. (See chapter 7.7 for further details).

It is interesting to note that according to Siegfried Sassoon's medal index card he was issued with a Silver War Badge once he had relinquished his commission on medical grounds but that his campaign medals were not issued until 1985, 18 years after his death.

For an act of gallantry performed as a result of enemy action, after his regiment had taken part in a trench raid on 25/26 May 1916 (WO 95/1665), Siegfried Sassoon was awarded the Military Cross (*London Gazette* 17 July 1916) for " conspicuous gallantry during a raid on the enemy's trenches. He remained for 1 and a half hours under rifle and bomb fire collecting and bringing in our wounded. Owing to his courage and determination all the killed and wounded were brought in." Note how this copy has been annotated with the date and place of the action.

Lond Gaz 27th July 1916.

near lip of enemy crater immediately the hostile mine had been exploded. E. of Mont St Eloy. 3rd & 8th May 1916

2nd Lt. Siegfried Lorraine Sassoon, 3rd (attd. 1st) Bn., R. W. Fus.

For conspicuous gallantry during a raid on the enemy's trenches. He remained for 1½ hours under rifle and bomb fire collecting and bringing in our wounded. Owing to his courage and determination all the killed and wounded were brought in. Fricourt 25/26 May 1916.

2nd Lt. Thomas Scott, 4th (attd. 1st) Bn., Sco. Rif.

For conspicuous gallantry. After the explosion of a mine he went out in daylight and endeavoured to reach an officer and man who were lying half buried below the lip of the

Fig 22 London Gazette entry for award of Military Cross to Siegfried Sassoon (WO 389/2)

According to his Military Cross index card (WO 389/21), Siegfried Sassoon had his Military Cross posted to him in January 1922.

Fig 23 Military Cross index card (WO 389/21)

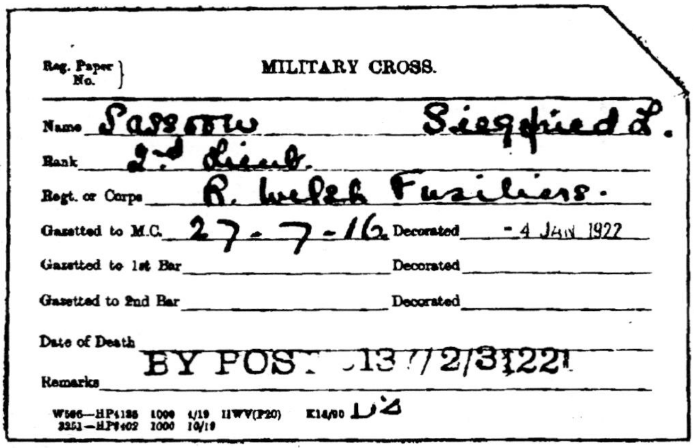

Reg. Paper No.

MILITARY CROSS.

Name Sassoon Siegfried L.

Rank 2nd Lieut.

Regt. or Corps R. Welsh Fusiliers.

Gazetted to M.C. 27-7-16 Decorated -4 JAN 1922

Gazetted to 1st Bar Decorated

Gazetted to 2nd Bar Decorated

Date of Death

Remarks BY POST 13/2/3122

W566—HP4136 1000 4/19 HWV(P20) K14/80
3351—HP4402 1000 10/19

Records of Service

As already discussed, the records of service can be found in two record classes: WO 339, with an index in WO 338, and WO 374. (See chapter 3)

The record of service for Siegfried Sassoon (WO 338/51440) contains his original attestation form when he joined the Sussex Yeomanry on the very day that war broke out, 4 August 1914 (fig. 24); the paperwork for his commission, the medical board records relating to his time at Craiglockhart (fig. 24) and other military hospitals, a copy of his open letter relating to the conduct of the war, which was read out in Parliament in July 1917 and a copy of *The Nation* containing verses by him.

Siegfried Sassoon's record of service is unusual primarily because of his activities in 1917. However, no two officer records of service are alike.

Army Form B. 201.

(Modified for use during Mobilization).

PLICATION FOR APPOINTMENT TO THE SPECIAL RESERVE OF OFFICERS.

The candidate will carefully complete the following particulars, obtain the certificates on page 3 and then

4828.

NOTED ON CARDS

11. 5. 15.

M. T. 3.

A Household Cavalry Regiment	The Officer Commanding the Regiment he wishes to join
The Foot Guards	
The Irish Horse	
King Edward's Horse	
A Cavalry Regiment	The Officer Commanding a Reserve Regiment of Cavalry, a Cavalry Depot, or the Officer in charge of Cavalry Records, Canterbury
A reserve unit of the Royal Garrison Artillery	The Officer Commanding the Reserve unit he wishes to join
A reserve unit of the Royal Engineers (see note (b) on p. 2)	
A reserve unit of Infantry	
The Royal Field Artillery	The Officer Commanding a Reserve Brigade or Depot
The Royal Garrison Artillery, but not to a reserve unit	The Lieut.-Colonel, Royal Garrison Artillery, in any Coast Defences, or the Officer Commanding a Depot
The Royal Engineers, but not to a reserve unit	The President of the Institution of Civil Engineers, Gt. George Street, Westminster, London, S.W., (unless the applicant be a member of the Senior Division of the Officers Training Corps, in which case the application will be forwarded direct to the War Office by the Adjutant of his Contingent.)
An Infantry Regiment, but not to a reserve unit	The Officer Commanding a Regular battalion or Depot of the Regiment he wishes to join
The Royal Flying Corps	
The Army Service Corps	Forward the application to—The War Office, London, S.W.
The Royal Army Medical Corps	
The Army Veterinary Corps	

If desirous of appointment to

Present himself in person to

1. Unit or branch in which the candidate desires to serve — 3rd Battalion. Royal Welsh Fusiliers.

2. Name of Candidate (in full) Surname ... Sassoon
   (See note (a) on page 2) Christian Names... Siegfried Lorraine

3. Date of birth — Sept. 8th 1886
   (A birth certificate or a baptismal certificate containing the date of birth to be attached or forwarded later.)

4. Whether married — No

5. Whether of pure European descent — Yes

6. Whether a British born or a naturalized British subject — British Born.

7. Whether the candidate has :—
   (a) Obtained a leaving or qualifying certificate as required of a candidate for admission to the Royal Military College under the regulations in force up to 1st April, 1912. (Certificate to be attached.) — No
   (b) Qualified at an Army Entrance Examination. (State date of examination.) — no
   (c) Passed the matriculation examination of a university, or a test accepted in lieu thereof. (Certificate to be attached.) — Yes.
   Or failing one of the above :—
   (d) Can produce a statement from the headmaster of a secondary school, or other competent educational authority, as to his educational attainments. (Statement to be attached.)

8. Permanent address — Weirleigh. Paddock Wood - Kent.

9. Present address for correspondence — Weirleigh

10. Profession or occupation — none.

11. Schools and Colleges at which educated — Marlborough College.

12. Whether now serving, or previously served, in any branch of His Majesty's Naval or Military Forces. If so, state :—
    (a) Regiment or Corps — Sussex Yeomanry.
    (b) Date of appointment — 4th August 1914
    (c) Rank — Private -
    (d) Date of retirement, resignation or discharge — Still serving
    (e) Circumstances of retirement, resignation or discharge
    (A Candidate who has served in the ranks should attach his discharge certificate.)

(8 8 10) 5000 8/14 H W V Forms
5000 9/14 B 201.

P.T.O.

Fig 24 Appointment of Lieutenant Sassoon to the Special Reserve of Officers (WO 339/51440)

ADMISSION AND DISCHARGE BOOK

_____ HOSPITAL

Index number of admissions. Transfers are not to be numbered consecutively with the admissions, but should be left un-numbered, or numbered in red ink as a separate series	Regiment, Battalion, Corps, or other unit	Squadron, Battery, or Company	Regtl. No.	Rank	Surname	Christian Name	Completed years of Age	Completed years of Service	Completed months with Field Force	DISEASES (Wounds and injuries in action to be entered according to classification on fly leaf)	Dat...
380^T	Lancs Fus.			Lt.	Crouchley	H.	21	2 $\frac{10}{12}$	$\frac{4}{12}$	Neurasthenia	10
381^T	17 att. 2/1 London			2 Lt.	Burk	K.	27	2 $\frac{9}{12}$	$\frac{5}{12}$	Neurasthenia	10
382^T	7 Yorks			Lt.	Sherwood	F.	32	14 yrs.	$\frac{8}{12}$	Neurasthenia	10
383^T	7 Yorks			2 Lt.	Harley	F.E.	34	1 $\frac{3}{12}$	$\frac{3}{12}$	Neurasthenia	10
384^T	R.S.			Cap.	Webb	M.W.T.	28	9	2 $\frac{8}{12}$	Neurasthenia	11
385^T	5th S.R.			2 Lt.	Clarkson	D.D.	30	2 $\frac{3}{12}$	1 $\frac{8}{12}$	Neurasthenia	13
✓ 386^T	H.A.C.			2 Lt.	Bosanworth	W.F.	21	1 $\frac{5}{12}$	$\frac{5}{12}$	Neurasthenia	13
387^T	R.F.C.			2 Lt.	Dubbridge	M.	19	1 yr.	$\frac{4}{12}$	Neurasthenia	14
388^T	10 att. 22 London Regt.			Lt.	Phillips	R.W.	23	2 $\frac{8}{12}$	$\frac{1}{12}$	Neurasthenia	14
389^T	21st Manchesters			2 Lt.	Whitworth	J.C.	29	5 $\frac{6}{12}$	$\frac{6}{12}$	Neurasthenia	14
390^T	R.F.a.			Lt.	Westwood	a.	36	1 yr.	$\frac{4}{12}$	Neurasthenia	14
391^T	2nd Yorks			Lt.	Bell	James	31	13 yrs	1 yr	Neurasthenia	16
392	1st Dorsets			Major	Hope	L.C.	44	20 $\frac{7}{12}$	1 $\frac{11}{12}$	Neurasthenia	14
393^T	11th Lon. att. R.F.C. (16 Sqdn.)			2 Lt.	Hale	H.R.	24	2 $\frac{9}{12}$	1 $\frac{2}{12}$	Neurasthenia	19
394^T	20th Manchesters			Capt.	Harford	J.F.	49	2 $\frac{5}{12}$	1 $\frac{3}{12}$	Neurasthenia	19
395^T	9th a.s.Ho			Capt.	Pillars, Ronald G.	28	2 $\frac{11}{12}$	$\frac{2}{12}$	Neurasthenia	21
396^T	5th Seaforths			2 Lt.	Macintosh	J.	26	5 yrs.	2 $\frac{3}{12}$	Neurasthenia	2
397^T	R.W.F.			2 Lt.	Sassoon, Siegfried		30	2 $\frac{11}{12}$	1 $\frac{1}{2}$	Neurasthenia	22
(28)	2nd R.S.			Major	Laidlaw	John	29	8 $\frac{4}{12}$	1 yr	Neurasthenia	Re-24
398	1/4 Oxford & Bucks			Lt.	Proctor	A.W.	34	2 $\frac{8}{12}$	$\frac{5}{12}$	Neurasthenia	25
399^T	2/7 K. Liverpools			Lt.	Boak	C.B.	32	2 $\frac{6}{12}$	$\frac{5}{12}$	Neurasthenia	25
400^T	R.F.a. 166 Bde.			Lt.	Wadman	C.R.	38	2 $\frac{7}{12}$	1 yr.	Neurasthenia	25
(157^T) }	13 Worcesters			2 Lt.	Hamm	B.J.	21	1 $\frac{6}{12}$	$\frac{3}{12}$	Neurasthenia	Re-25
401^T	R.F.a.			Maj.	Farrant	M.	31	10 $\frac{7}{12}$	2 $\frac{11}{12}$	Neurasthenia	25
402^T	7 Yorks, London Regt.			2 Lt.	Syre	Chas.	19	1 $\frac{5}{12}$	$\frac{7}{12}$	Neurasthenia	25
403^T	2/2 Lincolns			2 Lt.	Denby	A.N.	33	2 $\frac{10}{12}$	1 $\frac{3}{12}$	Neurasthenia	25
404^T	R.F.a.			Cap.	Shore	C.M.S.	24	2 $\frac{11}{12}$	1 $\frac{11}{12}$	Neurasthenia	25
405^T	2/10 London			2 Lt.	Morgan	W.	19	2	$\frac{6}{12}$	Neurasthenia	25
406^T	R.a.M.C.			Cap.	Ferguson	R.L.	36	1 $\frac{1}{2}$	1 $\frac{1}{2}$	Neurasthenia	25
407^T	A.S.C. (M.T.)			2 Lt.	Myers	L.S.	23	2	$\frac{7}{12}$	Neurasthenia	2

Fig 25 Craiglockhart Admission register (MH 106/1887)

FIELD SERVICE

Date of Admission		Date of Discharge			Date of Transfer				Number of days under treatment	Number or designation or ward in which treated	Religion	OBSERVATIONS
For original disease	By new disease supervening	To Duty	By new disease supervening	By Death	To		From					Number and page of case book to be quoted for all cases recorded in it. In transfers the designation of the hospital or sick convoy, to which or from which transferred, must be noted here, and any other facts bearing on the man's destination; also in moveable field hospitals the place where the admission, &c., took place should be indicated. Place of action to be noted in case of wounds and injuries received in action.
					Sick Convoy	Other Hospitals	Sick Convoy	Other Hospitals				
10 7/17		13 11/17						4th Lon.Gen. 116			C/E	
10 7/17		12 8/17						" 43			C/E	
10 7/17		11 8/17						" 32			C/E	
10 7/17		26 8/17						" 49			Pres.	
11 7/17		17 7/17 D.M.W.						Catchmore 66			C/E	
13 7/17		27 12/17 D.M.U						York Hill 164			Pres.	
13 7/17		10 10/17 D.M.W.						Dundee War H. 89			Pres.	
14 7/17		31 10/17 D.M.W.			18-7-17 Brad hill			4 Lon.Gen. 109			C/E	
14 7/17		23 11/17 D.M.W.						" 162			B'tist	
14 7/17		23 10/17						" 101			C/E	
14 7/17		11 9/17						2nd Western Gen. Manchester 59			C/E	
16 7/17		17 7/17 + D.M						York Hill 6			C/E	
14 7/17		10 8/17						4 Lon.Gen. 184			C/E	
14 7/17		15 4/17 D.M.W.						" 109			C/E	
14 7/17		28 8/17			24-7-17 Brad hill			" 40			Pres.	
21 7/17		12 9/17						Manchester 4th West.Gen. 53			Pres.	From H.S.
23 7/17		26 8/17						Craig Leith 218 23-5-17			Pres.	
23 7/17 Re-ad.		26 11/17 To Duty						1st Lon.Gen. 124 22-3-17			C/E	From L. duty.
24-7-17		7 7/17 H.S.						C.W.H. 14			C/E	From duty.
25 7/17		28 7/17 D.M.U						4th Lon.Gen. 218			C/E	
25 7/17		3 8/17 D.M.U						" 162			C/E	
25 7/17 Re-ad.		7 4/17			10-8-17 Re-admitted	30-12-17		" 105			C/E	
25 7/17		17 10/17 D.M.W.						" 84			C/E	
25 7/17		2 10/17			27-7-17. Coldstream M			" 69			C/E	
25 7/17		18 8/17						" 55			C/E	
25 7/17		11 8/17						" 105			C/E	
25 7/17		4 9/17 To Duty						" 48			C/E	
25 7/17					Foxley Aux Hos. Faux Thornadill 7-11-17			" 105			C/E	
25 7/17		7 9/17			Roy. Lancs. Hos. Blackpool			" 44			Cong.	
25 7/17		27 11/17						" 125			C/E	

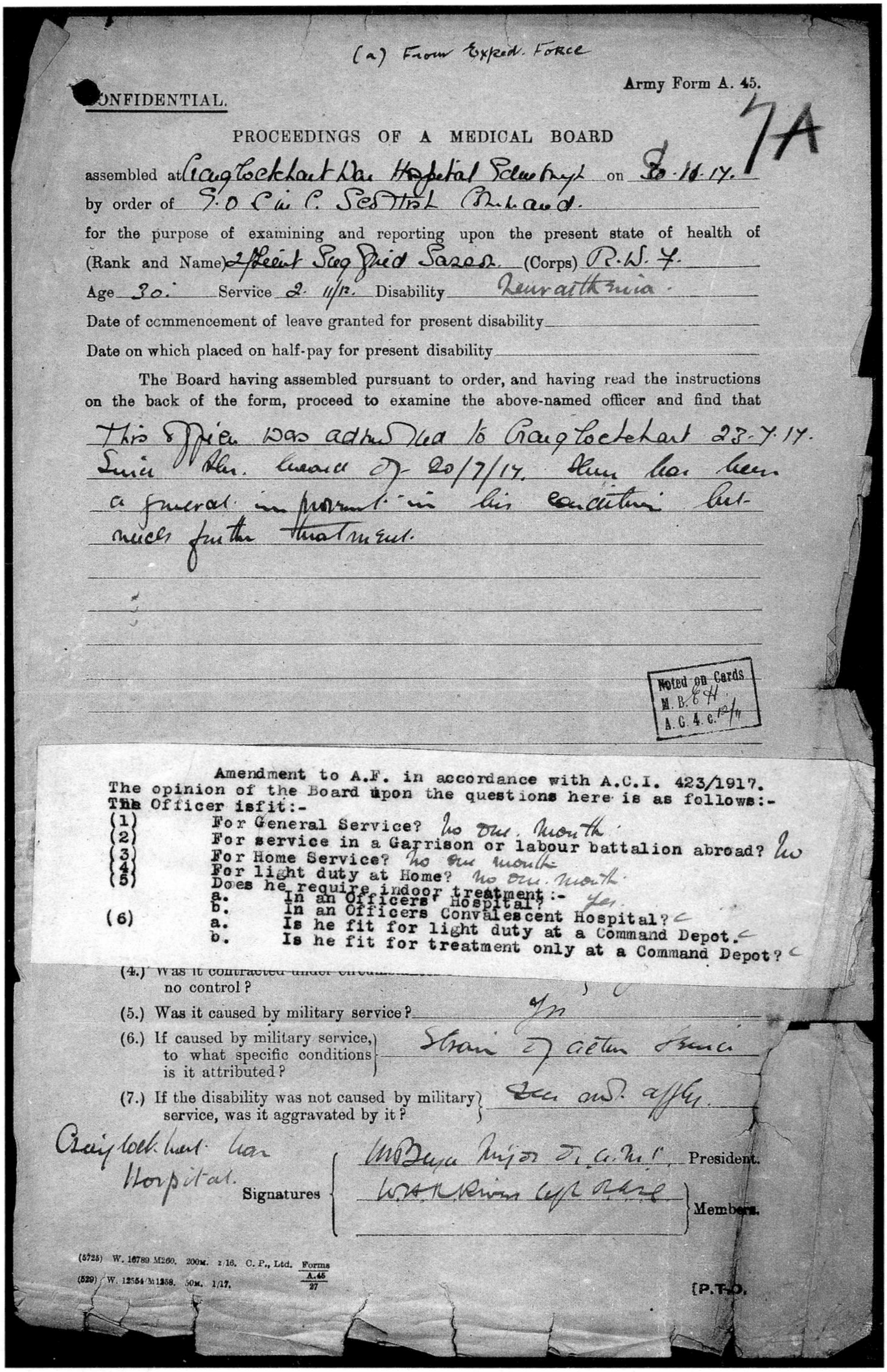

(a) From Exped. Force

CONFIDENTIAL.

Army Form A. 45.

7A

PROCEEDINGS OF A MEDICAL BOARD

assembled at Craiglockhart War Hospital Edinburgh on 20.10.17.

by order of G.O. Cu. C. Scottish Command.

for the purpose of examining and reporting upon the present state of health of

(Rank and Name) 2 Lieut. Siegfried Sassoon (Corps) R.W.F.

Age 30. Service 2 1/2. Disability Neurasthenia.

Date of commencement of leave granted for present disability _____

Date on which placed on half-pay for present disability _____

The Board having assembled pursuant to order, and having read the instructions on the back of the form, proceed to examine the above-named officer and find that

This Officer was admitted to Craiglockhart 23.7.17. Since then examined on 20/7/17. There has been a general improvement in his condition but needs further treatment.

Noted on Cards
M.B. 64
A.G. 4. c.

Amendment to A.F. in accordance with A.C.I. 423/1917.
The opinion of the Board upon the questions here is as follows:-
The Officer is fit:-
(1) For General Service? No one month.
(2) For service in a Garrison or labour battalion abroad? No
(3) For Home Service? No one month.
(4) For light duty at Home? No one month.
(5) Does he require indoor treatment:- Yes.
    a. In an Officers' Hospital?
    b. In an Officers Convalescent Hospital?
(6)
    a. Is he fit for light duty at a Command Depot?
    b. Is he fit for treatment only at a Command Depot?

(4.) Was it contracted under circumstances ... no control?

(5.) Was it caused by military service? Yes

(6.) If caused by military service, to what specific conditions is it attributed? Strain of active service

(7.) If the disability was not caused by military service, was it aggravated by it? See ans. above.

Craiglockhart War Hospital.

Signatures { M Bryce Major R.A.M.C. President.
W.A. Brown Capt. R.A.M.C. Member. }

(5725) W. 16780 M260. 200m. : 16. C. P., Ltd. Forms
(529) W. 12554 M1358. 50m. 1/17.

A.45
27

[P.T.O.

Fig 26 Medical Board Proceedings regarding Sassoon (WO 339/51440)

Bibliography

The bibliography below lists some of the books previously mentioned and others that we feel may be of interest.

Many of the books listed below are on sale in the PRO bookshop.

Abbott, P.E. and Tamplin, J.M.A.	*British gallantry awards.*	London: Nimrod Dix, 1981
Beckett, Ian and Simpson, Keith	*A Nation in Arms: A Social Study of the British Army in the First World War.*	Manchester University Press, 1985 and Tom Donovan, London, 1990
Brown, Malcolm	*The Imperial War Museum Book of the First World War.*	Sidgwick and Jackson, London, 1991
Colwell, Stella	*Dictionary of Genealogical Sources in the Public Record Office.*	Weidenfeld and Nicolson, London, 1992
Coombs, Rose E.B.	*Before Endeavours Fade: A Guide to the Battlefields of the First World War.*	7th edition, After the Battle, London, 1994
Cox, Jane	*New to Kew: a first time guide for family historians at the Public Record Office.*	PRO Reader's Guide No 16, 1993
Cox, Jane and Padfield, Timothy	*Tracing your ancestors in the Public Record Office.* (Public Record Office handbook no. 19: fourth edition by Amanda Bevan and Andrea Duncan) - A new edition of this work is in preparation, to be published by PRO Publications in November 1998.	London: HMSO, 1990 (4th ed.)
Department of Printed Books, Imperial War Museum 1989	*Gallantry awards of the British Army.* *(other than the Victoria Cross)* (DPB Booklist no. 53)	London: Department of Printed Books, Imperial War Museum,
Department of Printed Books, Imperial War Museum	*The Victoria Cross.* (DPB Booklist no. 77)	London: Department of Printed Books, Imperial War Museum, 1989

Hamilton-Edwards, Gerald	*In search of army ancestry.*	London: Phillimore, 1983
Fowler, Simon	*Army Records for Family Historians.*	PRO Readers' Guide No 2, 1992
Gilbert, Martin	*First World War Atlas.*	Weidenfeld and Nicholson, London, 1989
Giles, John	*The Western Front: Then and Now.* [One of a series about battlefields of the First World War]	After the Battle, London, 1995
Hallows, Ian S.	*Regiments and Corps of the British Army.*	London: Arms and Armour Press, 1991
Haythornthwaite, Philip J.	*The World War One Source Book.*	Arms and Armour Press, London, 1992
Holding, Norman	*The location of British Army Records 1914-1918: a national directory of World War I sources.*	Birmingham: Federation of Family History Societies, 1991 (3rd ed.)
Holding, Norman	*World War I army ancestry.*	Birmingham: Federation of Family History Societies, 1991(2nd ed.)
Holding, Norman	*More sources of World War I army ancestry.*	Birmingham: Federation of Family History Societies, 1991(2nd ed.)
Lake, Fred H.	*Regimental journals and other serial publications of the British Army, 1660-1980: an annotated bibliography in 4 volumes.*	London: Ministry of Defence, Whitehall Library, 1985
Saul, Pauline and Markwell, F.C.	*The Family Historian's enquire within.*	Birmingham: Federation of Family History Societies, 1991 (4th ed.)

Simkins, Peter	*Kitchener's Army.*	Manchester University and Tom Donovan, London, 1990
Watts, Michael J. and Watts, Christopher T.	*My ancestor was in the British Army: how can I find out more about him?* (My ancestor series).	London: Society of Genealogists, c.1992
White, Arthur S.	*A bibliography of regimental histories of the British Army.*	London:London Stamp Exchange 1988 (rev.ed.)
Williamson, H.J.	*Collecting and researching the campaign medals of the Great War.*	St.Margaret's, Norfolk: H.J. Williamson, 1990
Wise, Terence and Wise, Shirley	*Guide to military museums: and other places of military interest.*	Knighton, Powys: Terence Wise, 1994 (8th rev. ed.)

There are a number of Internet sites dedicated to the First World War. One of the most interesting is Trenches on the Web whose URL is: **http://www.worldwar1.com/**.